Women, Design,
and
The Cambridge School

A History of the Smith College
Graduate School of Architecture
and Landscape Architecture
in Cambridge

Henry Atherton Frost
1883-1952
Director of The Cambridge School, 1916-42

Women, Design, and The Cambridge School

DOROTHY MAY ANDERSON

PDA PUBLISHERS CORPORATION

Additional copies may be ordered from:
PDA PUBLISHERS CORP.
Box 3075
West Lafayette, Indiana
47906

Copyright © 1980 by Dorothy May Anderson

Library of Congress Catalog Card Number: 80-81341

ISBN 0-914886-10-X

Printed in the United States of America

*To all the women who studied
at The Cambridge School*

Contents

Preface

The Committee for Women in Landscape Architecture, a committee of the American Society of Landscape Architects (ASLA), is responsible for the initiation of this book. Over the luncheon table one spring day in 1975, I discovered that some of its members knew very little about their predecessors in the earlier part of this century and knew nothing at all about The Cambridge School, which had played an important part in my life. The outcome of our casual conversation was that the committee asked me to write a history of women in landscape architecture. Knowing that I had neither the background nor the fortitude, to say nothing of time, to embark on such a comprehensive project, I declined. I did, however, offer to write something about The Cambridge School and its puzzling relationship to Smith College. Little did I know then what I was undertaking.

I had been a student of landscape architecture at The Cambridge School in the early 1930's and on finishing my studies there had taught at The Lowthorpe School of Landscape Architecture in Groton, Massachusetts. Later, I had gone to Smith College as a member of its faculty and as the resident landscape architect in charge of redesigning the campus. At the same time, I had been a special critic at The Cambridge School. Thus, I had been a part of both Smith College, in Northampton, Massachusetts, and its small Graduate School of Architecture and Landscape Architecture in Cambridge during a rapidly changing and fairly critical period in the lives of both. While I had lived in and near Cambridge, I had haunted the Harvard libraries and in the summer of 1942 had studied at the Graduate School of Design. I was familiar with Harvard Yard and the role of women there in both a literal and a figurative sense. For all these reasons, I thought I could contribute something to the record of women in architecture and landscape architecture, perhaps one small facet of history that might otherwise be lost. The result of my decision to do so is this history of a small school of architecture and landscape architecture, which though excellent in its approach and performance, died a sudden death through lack of vision as well as the usual lack of funds.

During the 1930's, it was my great privilege to work closely with two distinguished men, William Allan Neilson, President of Smith College, and Henry Atherton Frost, Professor at Harvard University and Director of The Cambridge School. Both men are of particular significance to the story of this small school that eventually became The Smith College Graduate School of Architecture and Landscape Architecture in Cambridge. Their students always called them Mr. Neilson and Mr. Frost, the slight formality of the time — no first names, no nicknames — stemming from respect rather than awe of a position or a person. Both men hated to be called "Professor." Much has been said and written about Mr. Neilson, very little about Mr. Frost. This book is in part a personal tribute to Henry Atherton Frost as well as a salute to the women who studied under him and who share my desire to recognize his great and unusual contribution to the progress of women in the design professions.

Anyone who ever studied under Mr. Frost would agree that he was a memorable teacher. Most of his life was spent at Harvard University, from the time he entered as a student in 1905 until his retirement as Emeritus Professor in the Graduate School of Design in 1949. He had begun his teaching career in the Department of Architecture in 1909. Over the years in the Harvard classrooms, he taught the basic principles of design and construction to many men. From 1915 through 1942, he taught those same principles to the women at The Cambridge School, his own brainchild just outside The Yard; and after 1942, when Harvard first admitted women to its Graduate School of Design, he taught both the men and the relatively few women enrolled there. He often spoke of a difference in approach in teaching men and women and of the relative strengths and weaknesses of each in professional training. All his students, however, benefited greatly from his rare gift of almost intuitively understanding the personal problems that affected the work of each individual. His interest in his students and their careers was an intrinsic part of his life. It was while he was on his way to visit a former Cambridge School student that he was killed in an auto accident in 1952. He was the spirit and the guiding light of The Cambridge School even before it had a name, and as it advanced through triumphs and adversities, he was unquestionably the leader of an informal experiment that eventually became a recognized institution.

Dorothy May Anderson

Acknowledgements

If my thanks to all the people who helped write this book were recorded, we would have another book as long as this one. I trust they recognize themselves in the groups below and will know that only space prevents my acknowledging each helping hand individually.

Without the continuous support, and often hard work, of the ASLA Committee for Women in Landscape Architecture, the project would never have gone beyond a bit of luncheon chatter. The membership of the Committee changed several times while the book was in progress. I thank all the members, wherever they are now. For the long hours of work contributed by local members, particularly vulnerable to appeals for help, special thanks must go to Debra Dale, Deborah Le Clair, Sally Schauman, Ronda Skubi, Virginia Woolridge, and Samuel B. Miller, the only man on our committee, who offered sound advice and helped in many ways. Very special thanks from all of us go to Darwina Neal. It was Darwina who supported the project from beginning to end, not just with continuous encouragement and wise suggestions but by meeting every emergency with a miracle of sorts. Help in typing appeared out of thin air when it was badly needed, petty cash was on hand when we knew there was none, and occasionally gourmet food was served to sustain the interest of the volunteers as well as their appetites.

Several members of the American Society of Landscape Architects, including George Yarwood, Jot Carpenter, Ray Freeman, Norman Newton, and Hubert Owens supplied information, criticism, and general encouragement. The staff at ASLA headquarters helped with the tedious detail.

Many former students of The Cambridge School, others connected with the school at different times and in various ways, as well as relatives of deceased alumnae wrote letters filling in gaps in available information. Henry A. Frost, Jr., supplied photographs and some of his father's notes. I am truly grateful to all, particularly Anita Rathbun Bucknell, Edith Cochran, Carol Fulkerson, Faith Bemis Meem, Cary Millholland Parker, Elizabeth Pattee, Eleanor Raymond, and Gertrude Sawyer.

Confirmation of dates and other details remembered only in a hazy way came from a surprising number of institutions, more widespread than I had anticipated. They include the Universities of Illinois and Ohio; Columbia, Cornell, and Temple Universities; Radcliffe, Simmons, Smith, Wellesley, and Vassar Colleges; the Rhode Island School of Design; the Dumbarton Oaks Library, as well as the Loeb Library and the Archives of Harvard University. I appreciate the time spent by individuals who recognized the need for accurate answers to my questions, though my small project may well have been only a minor part of their day's work.

Most of all I am indebted to the Smith College Archives, keeper of the official records of The Cambridge School and keeper of the keys to much other pertinent information. I am especially appreciative of the personal help given me by Mary Bartram Trott, Assistant Archivist. When I think of Smith College, I think particularly of my former colleagues Charlotte Baum, Dorcas Brigham, W. I. P. Campbell, Erna Huber, Florence Macdonald, and Priscilla Van der Poel, and I thank them for sharing their memories of events related to The Cambridge School.

Thanks beyond measure go to Richard T. Allan and Norman T. Newton, who combed the final draft assiduously, and to Nancy Middleton, who typed the final manuscript.

Finally, I cannot ignore the patience of my cousins and the many personal friends who read and reread preliminary drafts, did the chores, helped with clerical work, and refrained from being too critical even when they obviously thought this book would never be finished. At long last, may they feel rewarded.

Introduction

by Darwina L. Neal, ASLA

In June of 1972, Raymond Freeman, President of the American Society of Landscape Architects (ASLA), speaking for the ASLA Board of Trustees, asked me to create a task force to investigate the status of women in landscape architecture. The initial response to a questionnaire sent to ASLA women in December 1972 was so overwhelming in its quantity and its depth of eloquent and sincere concern, that the survey was expanded to include non-ASLA women as well. The results of those surveys and task force recommendations for ASLA action programs which would create a greater awareness not only of the past and current contributions of women to the profession of landscape architecture but also of the full extent of their capability for further involvement were published in the July 1973 ASLA Bulletin on "Women in Landscape Architecture."

The task force was converted to a six-member ASLA Committee on Women in Landscape Architecture, which I chaired, to implement the recommendations. One of those recommendations was that ASLA sponsor the compilation of a comprehensive history of women in the profession of landscape architecture. Because of Dorothy May Anderson's expressed interest in the work of the Committee, we asked her to attend one of our committee meetings to seek her help. We were fascinated by her reminiscences of The Cambridge School and early women practitioners. Although we were unable to persuade her to undertake a history of women in the profession, she did agree to write the story of The Cambridge School.

To begin our project, we decided to send a questionnaire to landscape architects who had attended The Cambridge School. While we were waiting for the questionnaires to come in, research on the story of the school progressed. Although we had intended to summarize the information from the questionnaires as a part of the book, eventually it became apparent that, although the questionnaires helped to substantiate and fill in gaps in information, the story of the school could stand alone. It seemed more valid to compare briefly in an introduction the Cambridge questionnaire responses and attitudes in relation to the results of the 1973 ASLA survey and the current status of women in the profession of landscape architecture.

According to Mr. Frost's various notes in regard to the first years of the School, "...A study of the period will show that there was a certain unrest among women, a desire to broaden their horizons and activities.... For a woman...to hold an ambition outside her family life was more unusual than it is today.... women were beginning to demand equal rights with their brothers." Yet he went on to state that in the school the average girl regarded work as a temporary vocation which would cease with marriage, and she wanted to learn items of information in the quickest possible time — and was impatient about principles.

The results of the questionnaire, however, contradicted Mr. Frost's implication that landscape architecture would be a temporary vocation to Cambridge School graduates. Of those fifty-nine who responded, thirty-two percent practiced full-time until they retired and thirty-three percent practiced part-time or alternated periods of full-time and part-time work. Only thirty-two percent practiced for less than one year or not at all, but half of them did volunteer work such as designing public building grounds, judging beautification contests, chairing garden committees for public and private organizations, and participating in garden club activities which utilized their professional skills. Reasons most often given for not practicing were family commitments to husband and children, husband's career, or needs of other family members.

The major difference between ASLA and non-ASLA respondents to the 1973 survey was that ten percent of non-ASLA women were employed in another field and thirty percent had either not practiced because of family responsibilities or were working from their homes on a part-time basis only. Five percent of the non-ASLA women had never practiced. Several who had left the profession to raise their families were seeking to re-enter. Others stated that they had no desire to begin working again but felt that they could take full advantage of their professional background and at the same time contribute to the quality of life in their communities by taking an active part in local planning and zoning boards and other community action programs.

Both The Cambridge School and 1973 survey responses echoed the feeling of one woman working part-time from her home who wrote, "I have found the profession a fine creative outlet for a happy marriage.

I graduated in the wrong decade to have made it a career, [but]. . . it has been a rewarding part of my life." In fact, almost all 1973 respondents would encourage young women to enter the profession because they felt that it was rewarding and fulfilling, adaptable to combining a career and family, and in general exhibited less discrimination than other design professions.

The majority of women responding to all questionnaires were engaged in private practice — sixty-six percent ASLA, forty percent non-ASLA, and forty-eight percent Cambridge. Although seventy to eighty percent of these in all cases were principals in their own firms, most had one-woman offices or employed only women. With the exception of one ASLA woman, only offices in which males were co-principals employed male landscape architects. The majority of Cambridge respondents who worked in private offices were employed by women. The percentage of respondents employed by governmental agencies ranged from twenty percent ASLA and seventeen percent non-ASLA to twelve percent Cambridge. Since Cambridge respondents cited agencies which refused to hire women, that percentage is most probably inflated by those who had government jobs only during the war years or depression.

The three major objections to hiring women which Mr. Frost encountered with his peers were that women (1) would disrupt morale in an office of men, (2) could not supervise construction, and (3) would take jobs to which men were entitled. The last is no longer a concern, but ASLA men responding to a follow-up to the 1973 survey still mentioned the first two as objections or disadvantages to hiring women.

Two-thirds of all respondents to the 1973 survey felt that they had experienced discrimination. Of those who said they had experienced none, one-third of both groups had their own offices, and several, such as students and those who had never practiced, attributed their lack of encountering discrimination to their lack of professional exposure. Types of discrimination most often cited were in regard to salary, unfair hiring and advancement, and degree of responsibility. Discrimination by co-workers and other professionals was more common than that by clients and contractors. Lack of opportunity for field supervision and travel were also mentioned as was discrimination in types of work assignments.

In contrast, forty percent of the Cambridge women did not even answer a question as to whether they had ever felt handicapped in a predominantly male profession. Only five percent of the respondents said they had felt handicapped, but others mentioned specific examples of discrimination elsewhere on the questionnaire. One woman who did not answer the question wrote that, "Anytime a man has taken my position, he has been paid more and had more help."

Another stated, "I had no difficulties — didn't talk much!"

Those who said they had felt handicapped as women mentioned specific instances in which they had been told by a private group and a local park department and by several federal agencies that they would not be hired because they were women. One woman who has her own firm has found it difficult to make the social contacts with male politicians, architects, and engineers necessary to get jobs and stated that government officials seem to be prejudiced against giving women principals contracts if men are available. She felt that "it is probably easier for a woman to get a job in an office where the principal has been able to compare the work of both male and female employees and learned that a woman can be satisfactory."

This imposed need for women to "prove themselves" was cited by a variety of respondents to *all* surveys. Most agreed with the Cambridge graduate with her own practice who felt handicapped in her earlier years, but "not so in later years, because architects, workmen and employers had learned that my training and experience had given me expertise of a reliable quality." Unfortunately, however, many women practitioners must still "prove themselves," unless other competent women have already "paved the way" with clients, professionals, officials, and contractors. This is in spite of the fact of the same graduate's statement that, "The women's movement has had no noticeable influence in the work of my office, except perhaps to give clients more respect for women professionals [and] make them less apt to question our ability just because we are women." Another said, "Women's lib has come 35 years too late, but it is making a difference. If men ignore you now, I think they have a little shame about it."

Mr. Frost felt that women were better than men in residential work because they had a flair for design related to human scale and paid more attention to detail. This was probably why he placed the original Cambridge School emphasis on domestic architecture and landscape architecture. However, even after the curriculum was changed to include the full range of practice of both professions, the impression persisted — and still does in some attitudes today — as described in a 1973 response: "There's a tendency for fellow workers and even clients to feel that women in the profession are only competent to do planting plans.... I have endeavored to participate in a wide range of projects to avoid becoming specialized for my own sake." Some used this perception for their own gains though, as did one Cambridge graduate in private practice who said, "In some ways it is an advantage being a woman in the profession because, in residential work, the landscaping seems to be the province of the wife and she finds it easy to talk to a woman about it." Another said, "Men think women know more about plant materials than men do."

In relation to the preceding comments, it is interesting to look back on Mr. Frost's perceptions in June 1941 when he reviewed the progress women had made and the wider range of their work, which provided ". . . a breath of fresh air from the field and a gradual opening of doors for professional women."

Regardless of how wide the doors were opened at that time, they were opened. The Cambridge School education gave its graduates a foundation on which to build careers that significantly contributed and responded to the needs of the times. This unique education not only prepared graduates for careers in the mainstream of the profession but also for work experiences peripherally related to what was conventionally thought of as landscape architecture. As one graduate wrote, "Due mainly to the training at The Cambridge School, especially by Mr. Frost, I entered the field with sufficient expertise and self-confidence to gain the respect of others with whom I worked — clients, architects, construction men, and landscape firms. The school had given us understanding and respect for the interrelation of all these groups. The profession is an exciting one as Mr. Frost and his teachers led us to believe. They would have kept the curriculum still out in front if they were running the school today."

The influence graduates of The Cambridge School have had on the profession and on society is difficult to measure, but their work has unquestionably broadened the profession and improved our quality of life. As one reminisced, "In the changes that have come about since we were at The Cambridge School, [such as] the increasing population pressures and the disappearance of open space near urban centers, the diminishing quality of the environment in some large areas has made this of concern to many people and I, personally, have not made much of a dent in it. I think Abraham Lincoln put it best when he said he wished it could be said of him that 'he plucked a weed and planted a flower wherever he thought a flower would grow.'"

Thus would we all wish! The legacy of The Cambridge School will continue through the work of its graduates and those who experience it, as well as through its story which has finally been told.

Darwina L. Neal, ASLA
Chair, ASLA Task Force on Women in
    Landscape Architecture (1972-1973)
Chair, ASLA Committee on Women in
    Landscape Architecture (1973-1976)

1

The Beginning

The Cambridge School. In the minds and memories of the women who studied there, it was always The Cambridge School, in spite of many changes in its official name. Almost synonymous with the name of the school was that of its first and only director, Henry Atherton Frost; indeed, it was often referred to as The Frost School. Not through long-range planning and general ideas about professional education for women was this school established, but rather because of an unexpected challenge to a young architect at Harvard who was assigned the task of tutoring a young woman. She was a very persuasive young woman named Katherine Brooks, who wanted to enter the Harvard School of Landscape Architecture and who could not legally be admitted at that time, the fall of 1915. So the experiment began most informally, with Henry Frost tutoring Katherine Brooks in the basic principles of architecture and landscape architecture in the living room of her home in Cambridge. It did not end there. In fact, the living room routine was short-lived, and by February 1916, five young women were studying hard in the offices of Henry Frost and Bremer Pond in the Brattle Building on Harvard Square. Commenting on this period some years later, Mr. Frost has been quoted as saying, "We had a school and were not aware of it."

Few records of the very early days of the school are now available. If it was operated as informally as conversations with some of the first students indicate, it is doubtful that complete accounts were kept at the time, and about 1920 some of the school records were lost. At odd moments in 1943, however, Mr. Frost noted many things he remembered about this period, obviously intending to continue his notes and, eventually, to write a complete history of The Cambridge School or his own memoirs. It is our loss that he never did. This collection of unorganized and unfinished notes is generally referred to

1

as an unpublished autobiographical manuscript of Henry Atherton Frost. Chapters I and II of this book draw heavily upon these notes for background information and quoted material.

The Cast of Characters

The other teaching half of the "we" mentioned above by Henry Frost was Bremer Whidden Pond, a landscape architect who had recently opened an office in Boston after working several years as an assistant to Frederick Law Olmsted. He and Henry Frost shared another office in Cambridge to be nearer their Harvard classrooms. They hoped their professional practice would progress smoothly and would prosper, and they were determined that their established office routine would not be disrupted by the tutoring assignment Professor James Sturgis Pray had asked Henry Frost to undertake. At that time, Professor Pray was Head of the Harvard Graduate School of Landscape Architecture. Bremer Pond was an instructor in that School. Henry Frost was an instructor in the Harvard Graduate School of Architecture, headed by Professor H. Langford Warren, and he was also teaching a course in architectural design to the landscape students. That these two young men could have been unaware that they were about to have a school on their hands, or in truth might already have one, can best be explained by Katherine Brooks Norcross, their first student. An excerpt from a letter she wrote on February 21, 1976, follows:

> "The School started this way. Early in 1915, a Radcliffe College graduate, I wished to become a landscape gardener. But the Harvard School of Landscape Architecture did not admit women. However, Mr. Pray, head of the school, thought there was a definite need. Two instructors, Mr. Frost and Mr. Pond, were also interested. Why did I not have Mr. Frost come to my apartment once or twice a week? A year's study of architecture was necessary, in any case. I lived with my parents at Riverbank Court, on the Cambridge side of the Harvard Bridge. So, in our living room, one mahogany bridge table was carefully spread with a steamer rug for protection (one travelled to Europe by sea), and on it reposed a good-sized replica of a Greek temple with Doric columns for me to copy. Another bridge table, with another steamer rug, was almost totally covered with my huge drawing board, the pens, pencils, erasers, etc. And importantly, the triangular ruler, with all its many subdivisions.

> "After a month or so, Mr. Frost said, 'Why don't you move to my office in the Brattle [Building], where two or three other students would like to join us? Mr. Pond and I think this is a futile performance here... where you can't sling

ink about and must gather up all the eraser crumbs so they won't fall into the Oriental rug.'

"So in the early months of 1916, there were five of us — Emily Gibson, from Utica, New York, who did not continue; Miss Iasigi, a Boston socialite; Miss Luscomb, already a young architect from Waltham, Mass.; Miss Christensen; and myself. I wrote down their names at the time, otherwise I would not have remembered now. I will be 84 in June!"

Abby Christensen, the Miss Christensen mentioned by Katherine Brooks, came from Beaufort, South Carolina. Even at this early date, the fairly wide geographical distribution of the first students is interesting. Apparently, it didn't take long for these dedicated young ladies to convince their instructors that they were not only serious but also quite able to undergo the training devised for them and that their group need not forever be referred to, as it was by some of the Harvard men, as "The Frost and Pond Day Nursery." According to Mr. Frost, it was Abby Christensen who first started calling it "The Little School." No official name was mentioned in an announcement sent out in May 1916. It merely advised recipients that for the academic year 1916-17 professional instruction in the theory and practice of Landscape Design and Domestic Architecture would be offered to a limited number of students in the offices of Henry A. Frost and Bremer W. Pond in Cambridge, Massachusetts. By fall, however, so many women had asked to join the small informal group that a formal curriculum was obviously needed, and one was worked out and put into effect at that time. Thus, the fall of 1916 is usually considered the founding date of The Cambridge School.

Mr. Frost's version of the earliest days of the undertaking that was to become The Cambridge School differs slightly from that of Katherine Brooks Norcross, not factually but rather in point of view. In 1943 he wrote:

"In the fall of 1915, in [an] almost pastoral scene from another age,[1]...an event occurred, in itself innocuous enough though disturbing to my youthful complacency, which was to change my course for the next quarter century. James Sturgis Pray...called me into his office to tell me that a certain young woman, a Radcliffe graduate who was to go to Lowthorpe the following year to study landscape architecture, had applied to him for permission to study architectural draughting at Harvard in preparation for this new venture — and of course to permit such a thing was quite impossible. He had so informed the young woman but had added that he had just the solution. One of his young instructors could tutor her in her home and give her the same instruction his men were

3

receiving...Of course I saw the blow coming as the tale unfolded, and I knew Mr. Pray was acting with the kindest motives toward me. There was nothing for it but to accept with the best grace possible. From the middle of October to Christmas I met Mr. Pray's young lady two or three afternoons a week in her Mother's living room — or did we call it a parlor in those days? [— where] we attacked the classic orders of Vignola, the bible of the architecture of the day.

"In December Professor Pray turned over to me some correspondence he had been carrying on with a young woman from Utica, New York, who had studied landscape architecture for two years and apparently wanted to add some architectural training. [Also,] a Smith College graduate had appeared on the scene, from what source I cannot remember. At about this time three young women, one a graduate of the Massachusetts Institute of Technology who was practicing architecture in Waltham, Mass., and two others, one from Beaufort, South Carolina, the other from Brookline, [Massachusetts], wanted to join us. Both were students at the Massachusetts Institute of Technology [who had] applied to Bremer Pond for help in solving their landscape ambitions, because the landscape department at Technology had been discontinued some years previously.

"These student inquiries caused Mr. Pond and me some concern. I had already decided that tutoring the Tuscan orders on a teetering card table in a lady's parlor produced a certain sense of unreality and indifferent draughting. I had told my student that if she wished to continue, it must be at a solid draughting table in my office...If I had expected this would end it all, and there is no proof that such was my motive, I sadly misjudged the modern young woman of that day. She accepted with commendable alacrity, kept strict office hours from nine to five daily, and gave me no peace if I did not appear regularly at least once a day for criticism and instruction. And to my surprise I discovered that she could draught, could discuss design problems quite as intelligently as my students at the College, had no difficulty in understanding our architectural jargon, and showed a surprising enthusiasm for her work.

"Teaching a woman to do what we had always considered a man's job was not the painful ordeal it had promised to be. Mr. Pond had kept track of our progress and shared my surprise, and so to both of us the next step seemed not unnatural. We agreed to take on the...new applicants, to give them draughting space, and to tutor them according to their several needs...In order to make this concession we had to take on an extra office, but we agreed to make what we considered, in our innocence, a stiff charge for our services, twenty-five dollars a month per student.

"And so on February 14, 1916, the offices of Frost and Pond at 209 and 211 of the Brattle Building, [No. 4 Brattle Street], took on a new activity, by the addition of six[2] student draughtswomen whom we had agreed to initiate into the mysteries of our two professions. Whether the actual school started on this date...or the preceding October when I undertook my first tutoring job is unimportant...."

The Little School Experiment

In reviewing events and attitudes of this early period, Mr. Frost went on to say that it was natural for an individual seeking an outlet for creative instinct to turn to Harvard, as it was a well-known institution. He added that it was equally natural for older teachers, absorbed in their work and bound by traditional administrative rules, to be quick to say, "No women admitted," and forget the whole idea. Professor Pray seemed to be cut from a different pattern. Whether his suggestions for tutoring stemmed from a keen interest in women's education or from a charitable desire to help augment the meager salaries of his instructors is hard to say. Henry Frost thought it probably was the latter, adding, "and that was very likely our strongest motive for taking these women into our office." He went on to say:

"In trying to determine why our first puny efforts continued and to a certain degree succeeded, it occurs to me that it may have been because none of us who taught in those early days were great designers. When the blind tries to lead the blind there may be stumbling, but for all that it can be a jolly company. And truly we who undertook to lead were blind. We were only a few years older than our first students, and we had not lived long enough to accummulate great experience or to temper our illusions.[3] A teacher overhears more of his students' comments than it is wise to admit.... About myself I overheard 'It's not that he knows so much, because he doesn't. It's his enthusiasm that gets you'. At first the remark incensed me...later on, as I became more human, it caused me much amusement.... Our 'little school' was a democracy in the true sense, [but] I seem to remember that we who taught were a little on the timid side."

Mr. Frost regretted that he was not a cartoonist. He noted that if he were he would have pictured himself and Mr. Pond, supposedly the leaders, with halters around their necks, being dragged from one obstacle to another. They felt "driven by the lashes of the students' discontent" when things did not turn out as planned and were "warmed by a reserved approval" when they did.[4] He attributed the success of the office experiment, and later of the school itself, in large part to the fact that the first students were all college women. He wrote:

> "We were fortunate from the start, because as teachers conditioned to graduate students in the Harvard Schools, we had here young women on the graduate level. That group of students of 1915-16 together with those who came to us in 1916-17 were the real founders of the school... [Had they] been of a different caliber, had they required pushing and pulling to make them work, had they permitted outside interests to take precedence over their work with us, we would have let their efforts go by default, with probably no remorse....But these students drove us....It became a competition as to who would think of the next step first. It is the perfect way for a school to start, because it assumes an organization that is alive from the bottom up...And no school dies if it is alive."

The last statement reflects Mr. Frost's thinking in 1916, without benefit of a crystal ball, rather than in 1943, when he was writing it. By then, events had proved that factors other than the intelligence and liveliness of students have some bearing on the life and death of a school. In any case, he thought that the small size of the early group, as well as its college background, had a beneficial effect on the experiment. He was amazed, however, that students who were eligible to enter the best technical schools in the country as candidates for professional degrees should prefer a small office "not to be recognized for a few years yet as even a school, and not for many years as a 'recognized' school." He surmised that even though "The Little School" could not offer degrees, it attracted youth in whom the pioneering instinct was strong, but he marveled that their more conservative parents also were apparently satisfied. At least they paid the bills. His explanation was:

> "By limiting the number of students we would admit, which was necessary because of our small quarters, and because fortunately we had no capital in the form of endowment to expand rapidly, we were able to choose our students with care...and we were young enough not to be hidebound in academic matters....[We didn't find it necessary then or] in later years to limit admissions by hard and fast rules....We painted the courses as difficult, the future of a trained woman as uncertain, and gave the impression that we were not at all certain the applicant was desirable....The student who was herself doubtful of her interest and enthusiasm faded away promptly. The determined student was not dismayed."

On Valentine's Day, 1916, the first day of teaching more than one student, a notice posted on the bulletin board announced classes in elementary, intermediate, and advanced design, intermediate and advanced horticulture, history, construction, freehand, modeling, and office practice. Even the two instructors thought it was quite a bit to attempt, although they had a little help from J. Selmer Larson,[5] a sculptor who taught clay modeling in his studio. A bit later another notice read:

> "No more problems in either design or construction will be given out until all the work which has been announced to date is satisfactorily completed in all courses. Any student may commence the new problems as soon as her work is finished to the satisfaction of Mr. Frost and Mr. Pond without waiting for the others."

The students shared about equally in the sin of unfinished work, and even then it was the technical work that suffered, not the design.

On May 1st, 1916, the die was cast. The announcement of classes for the academic year 1916-17, mentioned earlier, was sent to various schools and colleges. Henry Frost and Bremer Pond, if not exactly trapped, at least could see which way the wind was blowing. Mr. Frost remembered the spring of 1916 as follows:

> "In February we disclaimed any plan for a school. . . . In May we sent. . . this announcement, which unless we were very naive, we knew committed us to at least a three-year program, and in the last analysis to an indefinite period. The time to stop. . . was then. If we had refused further registrations, if we had told our group that after June 1st we would not continue, the experiment would have ended there. We were encouraged in not making this decision by both Professor Warren and Professor Pray, two splendid teachers who rarely saw eye to eye, but in this instance did."[6]

"The Little School" was about to become more formalized, although it still had no official name. Some flexibility in the length of time required to complete the course was insured by consideration of previous training and demonstrated ability, but it was stated that normally the course would cover three years. The goal was to be achieved through "lectures, conferences, observations, tests, and desk work." The number of classes to be taught by Mr. Frost and Mr. Pond is astounding, and soon they admitted that only unbounded enthusiasm could have blinded them to the physical impossibility of doing so many things at once. Their plan included other lecturers and practitioners, but as time went by it was the number of these "others" and the need for money to pay them that endangered the equilibrium of the ambitious undertaking.

In May 1916, when the first announcement about professional instruction was circulated, less than a year had gone by since the first tutoring lesson, a busy time for all concerned. Before continuing the story of the school after it became a school, not just a group, it may be helpful to recall something of the professional climate of 1916, in which the two young instructors were operating. It is doubtful that they were interested only in making a little extra money for themselves, as Mr. Frost suggests. They were busy not only with "The Little School" and their office practice but also with their teaching responsibilities at Harvard. Mr. Frost remembered that period in his 1943 comments on the Graduate School of Architecture and the Graduate School of Landscape Architecture of Harvard.

> "The two schools, although housed in the same building [Robinson Hall], had at that time, and indeed for many years later, almost nothing in common. There was little or no exchange of ideas, no cooperation or collaboration.... Architecture in the United States had taken on a professional status from two main sources: the historical, as demonstrated at Harvard and a few other schools, or the Ecole des Beaux-Arts, as demonstrated at the Massachusetts Institute of Technology. Where the Beaux-Arts influence prevailed, the engineering side of the profession was likely to be strong. Where the historical approach was strong, association with the fine arts dominated. Gradually these sources merged.... Landscape architecture, on the other hand,... sprang directly from a study of plant materials, plant design, and horticulture. Not infrequently, schools of landscape architecture were departments in schools of agriculture....

> "There had been a growing belief among the younger group of practitioners and teachers that architecture and landscape architecture and structural engineering were not three separate compartments...but were in reality three components of a single design effort which included site and shelter.... There were architects who claimed the landscape architect must stop at the house terrace and must do no minor structures that related to his design. Landscape architects claimed that their work went properly to the walls of the building and they must do [all] minor structures [such as] steps, terraces, ramps, pools, etc. that entered into their design effort. Moreover, I remember their claim that they must be first on any job to place the building and orient it, but incongruously enough, it did not seem to bother them particularly if the architect designed the building before they picked the site. Even to us who had been trained in these traditions the arguments did not make sense. With a fine disregard for professional squabbling,

we argued that a design was made up of exteriors and interiors, of volumes and spaces, that these should be controlled by a single designer, [and] that if he were capable it mattered little to us what he called himself. Actually, I suppose, we were unconscious pioneers in a more modern and reasonable approach to the problem of design. To our elders...we were young radicals who had not profited from their training. At least we were in the pleasant state of being able to argue and criticize without responsibility. Our elders controlled the situation....

"Doubtless teachers of our generation were agitating similarly in other long-established schools, where definite traditions had been built up laboriously over the years, where the elders moved only after long and careful deliberation....[For our experiment,] we were fortunate in our youth....We had no past, no older and wiser faculty members to advise us and to dictate. We were not part of a great institution and as one of its parts required to consider our decisions in relation to the organization as a whole. We travelled light, and so could move with speed. A decision in the evening could be put into effect in the morning. If, on trial, it proved to be mistaken, in twenty-four hours it could be changed and we were off on another tack. Unstable, you will say. Quite. But we must remember that youth was leading youth, and for them instability, change, and progress are terms likely to be easily confused. In my later years I marvel at our temerity. At the time, it worked and was exciting for both students and teachers. That it succeeded was due largely to the fact that the students thought of the school as their own. There are worse things for a school than financial poverty....A study of the period will show that there was a certain unrest among women, a desire to broaden their horizons and their activities. This had been developing gradually,...[but] in 1915-16 the plight of the average girl who aspired to what were considered men's careers was not enviable....We were too young to have a mature judgment of the educational and social changes that were going on quietly....We had had no training that helped us to understand that we had quite by chance been caught up in a small eddy of a greater movement in which women were beginning to demand equal educational rights with their brothers."

Thus it was this kind of thinking and differing attitudes that prevailed during 1915 and 1916. Harvard's President Lowell was never very enthusiastic about the experiment in which his young instructors indulged themselves. He said that it would not succeed, because it had "no basis for continuity," which Mr. Frost explained, was merely

Bostonese for "no money." But Mr. Frost went on to say, "What he overlooked was that if by some mischance you grab a bull by the tail, and the bull resents it, there will undoubtedly be continuity so long as strength continues or until help arrives...We had put ourselves in such a predicament...Between October 15, 1915, and February 14, 1916, I suppose the tutoring of a single student at twenty-five dollars a month must have brought into the office coffers about seventy-five dollars. What became of such a princely sum I cannot remember."

At the end of the experiment's first fiscal year, September 1916, the Frost and Pond office opened a separate account for the school, in which they deposited $1,159.00. A bill for $139.25 still had to be paid. Whatever tuition fees were received during the spring and summer terms had gone for equipment, supplies, printing, and general overhead. The two instructors had allowed no salaries for themselves. In looking back from a very different perspective in 1943, Mr. Frost summed up the situation at the end of the school's first year by noting that "teachers are a little queer." Had he followed through on his metaphor of the bull, he might have added that in the quarter-century history of The Cambridge School, strength definitely continued, and help arrived eventually, albeit often just in the nick of time.

---

[1] It seems odd to think of Harvard Yard at any time as a "pastoral scene from another age," but a short excerpt from Mr. Frost's 1943 notes provides a general setting for the period as follows: "In 1915 the first World War was well underway, but to most of us it meant only newspaper headlines. The automobile was still a luxury...In 1911 I had travelled...ten miles to my wedding, with a hack and a pair of horses...In that same year, my wife and I had hurried to Atlantic [Massachusetts, now part of Quincy,] to see Grahame-White, a noted English flier, take off in what can properly be called a crate to fly to Worcester, Mass., circle the city hall, and return to the improvised flying field...We lived in quiet contentment without the radio...The males still affirmed stoutly that women's place was in the home, but the women, perhaps wiser than their mates and seeing the future more clearly, appeared to acquiesce while they never bothered to affirm."

[2] Mr. Frost remembers the group as six women; Mrs. Norcross names only five, including herself. Memories are faulty. It is possible that the Smith College graduate who appeared on the scene from limbo, as it were, disappeared just as mysteriously. It is more likely that Eleanor Raymond, a graduate of Wellesley College, was remembered as the sixth student. Certainly she was part of the very early group, but she herself believes that she joined it later in 1916. No registration records earlier than 1919 are available, and none of these slight discrepancies seems to matter much in the story of a group that was growing like Topsy before it was formally recognized as a school.

[3] While looking over old records in 1943, sometime after he made this comment on relative age, Mr. Frost was astonished to find that a few of the early students had been graduated from college a year or two ahead of him and that several were about his own age.

[4] At times positions were reversed and the students, who also felt driven, had their egos wounded by some disappointment they felt was not entirely justified. Some of the earliest students still remember that the motherly person who helped put them back together again after a personal crisis and who shared their thrills when achievement exceeded expectations was Miss Nellie Carpenter, a public stenographer whose office was just across the hall from Frost and Pond. She was equally friendly and resourceful when the young professors needed help. It is doubtful that she wholly shared the dreams

10

of a bright new future for women in any profession, but as so often happens when the right person is in the right place at the right time, she renewed her neighbors' faith in human nature as she shared their personal enthusiasms and troubles.

[5]The spelling of J. Selmer Larson's name varies considerably in early records, sometimes hyphenated, sometimes not, sometimes Larsen. Mr. Frost, in his manuscript, usually spoke of him as Mr. Larson.

[6]Henry Frost considered H. Langford Warren his greatest teacher. At the end of a long tribute to Professor Warren's ability to make history come alive for his students, he said: "A great teacher, too sincere to be a showman, [he was] a little man with a tuft of hair that gave him somewhat the look of a cockatoo, a reddish round beak, and a monumental impatience, which flowed from boundless energy; and withal one of the kindliest of men. His lectures always began promptly but rarely ended on the hour. . . . We poked fun at him, we cartooned him, but we loved him." Regrettably, we have no such colorful sketch of the more even-tempered and dignified Professor Pray.

2

The Early Years

When the fall term of the nameless school opened on September 18, 1916, nine students were enrolled. Two were from the original group, two from the summer term, and five were new. Three others registered a bit later, so the enrollment for 1916-17 was officially twelve, or double the size of the first group. Aside from having no official name, the experiment had no recognizable link to the outside world other than the May announcement and a circle of personal contacts that was growing wider every day.

Curriculum and Faculty

It did have an ambitious curriculum, and the faculty of four considered themselves lucky that only eleven of the sixteen courses announced need be given that year, because no students were yet prepared for advanced work. Mr. Frost and Mr. Pond shared the teaching of design, construction, history, and horticulture. Martin Mowrer, recruited from Harvard, taught freehand drawing; and J. Selmer Larson continued his Saturday classes in clay modeling. The school also offered a course in town planning and urban housing, which was taught by Professor Pray.[1] Abby Christensen, one of the two students from the first group, was the first woman to do any teaching — officially. While continuing her studies, she worked part of the time as an assistant in the drafting room. Unofficially, as Mr. Frost has said over and over again, through the years the students taught each other and their teachers all the time.

The young ladies had made their point within a year. They were capable of being trained as professionals. As the need for help with the teaching load increased, the instructors seem to have pressed into service six of their Harvard colleagues, including Martin Mowrer, as well as some outsiders. The two "young radicals" could not have been truly ostracized by their more conservative elders, because twenty special lectures were given by Harvard professors during the academic year 1916-17. That one of the special lecturers was H. Langford Warren, the forceful and scholarly Head of the School of Architecture, and another James Sturgis Pray, the man of vision who was Head of the School of Landscape Architecture, seems remarkable indeed. It testifies to their interest in the great experiment of teaching women in these two professional fields. Of the twenty lectures given to the students of "The Little School" that year, two by Professor Warren were on architectural history,[2] and three by Professor Pray on town planning. Henry V. Hubbard gave six lectures on landscape design, Charles W. Killam four on construction, and Stephen F. Hamblin five on plant materials. Also, William S. Ball lectured on wood finishes, and Walter G. Ball on stained glass. Since the total financial outlay for all instruction for the year was $905, none of these men could have charged exhorbitant fees. Mr. Frost remembered particularly the generous help of Mr. Larson in clay modeling and in his 1943 notes remarked that because the earliest school records were lost, what they paid him was "a matter of conjecture. . . better not pursued."

Precedents Set in 1916-17

Several precedents were set during this first official year. The instructors not only took the students to local industries and nurseries to study first hand the materials that were related to their problems, but they also organized longer study trips to Newburyport and New York. During this first year, the nameless school held its first exhibition that was open to the public. This was a collection of large photographic enlargements of the work of the architectural firm of Duhring, Okee and Zeigler of Philadelphia, a firm well known for residential design and very much in favor in academic circles at the moment. It is probably safe to assume that much of the "public" came from the Schools of Architecture and Landscape Architecture at Harvard.

Another precedent destined to recur periodically was the acquisition of more working space. The students felt cramped in the two offices in the Brattle Building, so another room was added to the office-school. Professor Warren had lent the school library — a "painfully small collection of books" — 450 architectural photographs. Fletcher Steele, a well-known landscape architect in Boston who had joined the Red Cross to do war work in Europe, lent his excellent collection of books on architecture and landscape architecture to the School for the duration of the war. Both collections benefited the students greatly, but they also took up space. Everything but the offices seemed to be increasing in size, even the deficit, which at the end of the year was $591, as compared to $139 the year before. There is no record of whether Mr. Frost and Mr. Pond paid themselves anything.

Perhaps the most noteworthy precedent of that eventful year, 1916-17, was the publication of a school catalog. Later, in 1943, Mr. Frost commented on the customary practice of schools sending out a yearly catalog of courses, with names of faculty members and any other pertinent information that applicants might want to know, adding "We did not follow this practice with meticulous regularity. Sometimes it took more than a year to recover from the pecuniary outlay involved." By spring 1917, however, some money apparently was available, the curriculum was fairly well set, as was the purpose of the school, which had been discussed at great length by all concerned.

So in March 1917 the school issued an eight-page catalog for the academic year 1917-18, listing twenty-two full courses, compared to sixteen the year before, as well as fourteen half-year courses. The catalog included the names of four permanent instructors — Frost, Pond, Mowrer, and Larson — and the names of all but one (William S. Ball) of the special lecturers mentioned before, who had lectured during the 1916-17 academic year. Two new names, Walter G. Thomas and William S. Brown, were added but with no more information than that Mr. Thomas was from Cambridge and Mr. Brown from Boston. A statement of the purpose of the school reads:

> "The purpose of the instruction is to train students of the architectural and landscape professions. The courses offered are a) the theory and practice of domestic architectural design, b) the theory and practice of landscape design with particular reference to domestic work, or c) the combination of these two in the study of the house and garden."

The cover of the catalog identified it as that of "The Cambridge School of Architectural and Landscape Design for Women." It is the first time this name for the school was used officially and probably the first time the experiment going on in the offices of Frost and Pond on Harvard Square was called a school. The catalog was printed on cream yellow paper rather than the sage green stock of the May 1916 announcement, and it is further identified as Bulletin No. 2, evidently considering the earlier announcement as No. 1.

Mr. Frost said that this catalog "was regarded by us all as a masterpiece of persuasive literature, just sufficiently imposing to intrigue the interest of the ambitious student while it dismayed the timid. As I look at it today (1943), with less prejudiced eyes, two things strike me. Apparently, we had the same faith in our printer that men sometimes display erroneously in their tailor; and certainly we were very brave or very stupid young men."

Still reminiscing, Mr. Frost spoke of what might seem to others to be discrepancies between the catalog descriptions and the actual situation. The students who elected to enter the group could tell at a glance that the school had no great wealth behind it, and they didn't care. Their director was apprehensive, however, when persons, particularly parents, came to Cambridge from some distance away to see the school.

> "The surprise of these visitors must have been acute, when they realized that two or three rooms housed all the activities our catalog portrayed. The surprising thing to me is that I do not remember...a single suggestion that we had used the mails to defraud. These good people accepted our poverty as of no importance, just as we did. They sensed...the spirit of the students, and condoned as immaterial the limitations of our surroundings. [At that time] I hoped that the school would never have quite enough money to do all the things it must do for its students.... And we were destined to have [that] wish in generous measure.... I am sure we taught no less well when there was not enough money in the treasury to pay the next month's rent, and when salaries were held up for lack of funds. And the plans we made for the use of the money when, if, and as it did come in were as inexhaustible as those of any prospector when pay dirt is running poorly and he dreams of a 'strike'."

Although the students of 1916-17 came from distinguished institutions — Smith, Wellesley, Radcliffe, Vassar, M.I.T., Abbott Academy, the Cathedral School of Girls, Finch, and Winsor — The Cambridge School of Architectural and Landscape Design for Women was not yet a graduate school, merely an informal organization offering professional training. It was "gradually drifting into a graduate school point of view," however, because of the background and training of its two leaders. They were somewhat concerned at first about the applicants who did not have college degrees, but they could see no good reason for refusing to accept them. Mr. Frost noted: "We found them willing workers, so apt in their ability to understand, that from this time on we welcomed such students in moderation, in fact took them eagerly." The "moderation" refers to the number accepted, not to a limited welcome. As the years went by, the instructors were convinced that the mixture of college and non-college women was an advantage to both, but they always tried to maintain a solid majority of college graduates. They recognized the fact that the high-school level background of the younger students was, through no fault of their own, inadequate to the graduate-level training offered. Had they taken in more than a few such students at a time, the work might have seemed too hard, if not impossible, and the courses would have had to be revised downward. In that case, the college graduates would have been dissatisfied. So, with their pick-

and-choose policy toward applicants, they were able to maintain the sort of mixture they thought was best for all. In 1943 Mr. Frost analyzed the situation thus:

> "For the college graduate the professional study was not particularly different from her four years at college, except that it was more intensive and more definitely limited in its objectives. To the preparatory school graduate it was a completely new and exciting adventure. The older students patronized the younger ones, perhaps, but they also looked after them, saved them from making foolish mistakes, helped them over the hard spots. It is quite possible for students to learn more from each other than from their teachers, and it is entirely natural for mature students to help the younger, to influence them, and in doing so to increase their own capacity. We often were surprised at the success of the preparatory school graduates, particularly in design."

Climate of the Times

Even with so favorable a combination of students and courses, the instructors thought the turnover of students during the first few years was excessive. Mr. Frost's 1943 explanation for this is a comment on the professional climate of the times.

> "The *average* girl, however serious she was in her work...regarded it as a more or less temporary vocation which would cease with marriage. She accepted an entirely realistic attitude that since she was training in preparation for a probably limited period of professional activity, she need not go as far in her training as her brothers. Primarily, she [wanted to learn] in the quickest possible time how to design and construct, and above all how to draught. If her interest was in landscape, she was concerned particularly with items of information and was sometimes impatient about principles. The student did not envision for herself a lifetime of professional activity in which she would accept and carry out commissions of heavy responsibility. Rather, she saw herself as an assistant in an office and was content with this view. That she could marry, bring up a family, and also practice as an independent architect or landscape architect did not intrigue her. I use the term 'average' advisedly, because from the first there were those hardy souls who insisted upon the entire training....

> "A student needs concrete evidence to stimulate imagination. As second- and third-year courses were developed so that the beginner could see the work being carried out well beyond her immediate ability, she naturally widened her range of interest. When later we began to show her the

work executed by graduates, again her imagination was fired to train herself to execute [such work]. For a woman, particularly in the earliest days of the school, to hold an ambition outside her family life was more unusual than it is today. It ran counter to the general attitude of the time."

Another explanation for the average student's acceptance of the future as a few years of minor work in an office and then marriage forevermore may well have been her own observation of what went on in the outside world. One of the basic tenets of the philosophy behind the training at The Cambridge School was that after completing three years of courses and problems the student would then spend three or four more years as an apprentice (paid, but not highly paid) in the office of some well-established architect or landscape architect before setting up her own private practice. In theory, this approach had much to recommend it. Actually, the earliest graduates of the School had great difficulty in obtaining jobs with architects and landscape architects, even though they were well trained. Mr. Frost personally tried to help them, to break some barriers for them, but he admitted that it was rough going. The two objections he encountered most frequently among his professional peers were that 1) a woman in a drafting force of ten to fifty men would disrupt the morale of the office [morale, not morals], and 2) a woman could not be used as a superintendent as easily as a man nor could she run the necessary errands to various fabricating plants connected with construction. On the latter count, Mr. Frost tried to allay the fears of his colleagues by telling them of all the quarries, brick kilns, lumber yards, and steel assembly plants his graduates had scrambled through and up and over, adding that "their agility on ladders and scaffolding and their intelligence in the many details of building construction" seemed to him to be commendable. Only time and experience could take care of the first count, but when a few jobs opened up and men and women worked in the same office, the fear of disrupted morale proved to be groundless. Mr. Frost remarked that "the women were not dangerous, nor were the men oversusceptible." He found the practicing landscape architects more cordial and receptive to the idea of hiring women than the architects.

The School itself was affected by the early graduates' search for jobs, and at one point Mr. Frost wondered if the utter lack of discrimination on the part of his faculty toward the students had helped or hindered them. The students had become so accustomed to being taken at their own worth, to being measured by what they could do, not whether they were men or women, that they found hunting for jobs discouraging. Within a few years the situation improved greatly, but of this passing phase Mr. Frost said:

"Because they could not find offices to take them in, . . . our students got into the habit of accepting commissions as practitioners without the benefit of...invaluable office training. As a result, the instructors in the school found themselves in a position of consultants and indeed tutors to these young practitioners during the earlier years. Whenever we could, those of us who had small offices used our own graduates as office assistants, but this took care of only a few of them. We did at one time consider seriously establishing a sort of clinic to which graduates could bring their jobs, work them out under our guidance, and pay a fee to the clinic for its support. The idea...had merit, but there were not enough hours in the day to do all the things we had to do, let alone taking on further obligations."

The faculty thought that matters might be improved by a little discreet publicity in the right places. They decided that a short article in the *American Architect*, a reputable magazine, could be illustrated with some of the students' work. At least,it could do no harm to either the School or its graduates and might help reduce the skepticism about women's ability in the profession. So Mr. Frost went to New York to interview the editor. This somewhat fiery gentleman with pronounced ideas welcomed his visitor kindly, listened sympathetically to the story of the young professional's problem, and indeed showed some enthusiasm about helping them. In his 1943 notes, Mr. Frost described the end of the conversation.

"Inadvertently, I mentioned that the students were all women. The explosion was immediate. My editor friend told me forcefully that he would not be guilty of lifting his hand to help the cause of women in any fields that belonged by rights to men. He harangued on the way women were forcing themselves into business and professional circles everywhere. One statement I have never forgotten, 'The subways of New York are filled with ticket-takers and track walkers who hold degrees from our leading law schools, and are forced to do such menial labor by the influx of women into their profession.' I was ushered out, or should I say driven, from his office with hardly an opportunity to pick up my hat."

The students were certainly aware of this widespread attitude, although they knew there were exceptions to it. Mr. Frost marvelled at their courage "in spending time and money so generously in training [themselves] for professions in which they were so definitely not wanted."

Perhaps it took no more courage to enter the professional world than to begin their training in the first place. Women who had preceded them in other schools also found it hard. Martha Brookes Hutcheson, one of the pioneers in the field, told Mr. Frost that in 1898 she walked around the block three times before she could bring herself to climb those awful steps to the Massachusetts Institute of Technology. Her parents had been scandalized by her decision to study landscape architecture. Using the carrot-and-stick philosophy, they had promised her a trip to Europe and had given her permission to do anything she liked to the family's country estate if she'd give up her fantastic idea of going to a technical school. At the same time, they warned that she would be socially ostracized and would bring dishonor on the family if she pursued her plan. Obviously, she pursued and persevered.

Beatrix Jones Farrand, another great pioneer in the profession, probably would not have been one of the eleven founders of the American Society of Landscape Architects in 1899 had she lacked courage to overcome some of the early obstacles. Later, she earned wide recognition and exerted great influence on the profession, though in 1894 Frederick Law Olmsted had referred to her as a person who was "supposed to be in some way inclined to dabble in Landscape Architecture."

Although the little group in Cambridge in 1916 formed the nucleus of the first graduate school of architecture and landscape architecture that was exclusively for women, these women obviously were not the first who wanted to become architects and landscape architects. Some, like Beatrix Farrand and Ellen Shipman, had trained themselves through unceasing and diligent study and a keen observation of the world around them. Mrs. Farrand had been encouraged and helped along the way by Charles Sprague Sargent of the Arnold Arboretum, and Mrs. Shipman by her friend Charles Platt, a distinguished architect. Others had knocked on the doors of the State universities and colleges that offered professional training and had been admitted, albeit reluctantly in some cases, since the late 19th century. The State-financed schools were legally obligated to take them if they qualified for entrance. The Cambridge School was unique in that it trained women separately in two related professional fields, as men were trained separately at some of the men's universities and colleges.

Relation to Other Schools

The Cambridge School was not the first, however, to offer training in landscape architecture to women only. In 1901, Judith Eleanor Motley Low, who had studied horticulture at Swanley College in England, founded The Lowthorpe School of Landscape Architecture, Gardening and Horticulture for Women. She converted her beautiful country home in Groton, Massachusetts, into a school as a memorial to her late husband, Edward Gilchrist Low. The unwieldy name of the school was later shortened to The Lowthorpe School. Mrs. Low's decision to open her own school was influenced primarily by the closing of the landscape department at the Massachusetts Institute of Technology in 1900, on the grounds that only one school, Harvard, was needed in the Boston area. In terms of area and population, this may have been sound reasoning; but in realistic terms, it deprived women of an opportunity to go to a school where they could study landscape architecture.

From the beginning at The Lowthorpe School, the major courses were landscape design, mostly in the English manner of Gertrude Jekyll, and construction. They were reinforced, however, by much more intensive courses in planting design, plant materials, horticulture, soils, and general garden maintenance than were available in other schools at that time. There was also a formidable array of minor subjects that were in some way related to gardening. Like The Cambridge School later on, The Lowthorpe School accepted both college graduates and women who had not attended college, but the curriculum was designed to be completed in two years, not three. Katherine Brooks' original plan in the fall of 1915 was to enter The Lowthorpe School after a year's study of architecture at Harvard, if Harvard would let her enter.[3]

In 1910, Jane Bowne Haines, a Bryn Mawr graduate, had founded the Pennsylvania School of Horticulture for Women in Ambler, Pennsylvania. Although from the beginning this school offered courses in landscape design (probably called landscape gardening), the emphasis was on horticulture and gardening. Its main purpose was to offer to American women a two-year course in horticulture that was comparable to the professional training available to women in Europe at that time.

The founders of The Cambridge School had the advantage of seeing what problems earlier schools for women had faced. The precedents set by The Cambridge School during its first academic year — special lectures, visits to local businesses and museums, study trips farther afield, public exhibitions, constantly improved facilities, and the publication of a school catalog — were all positive steps beneficial to the School throughout its life. Part of the text of the first catalog, however, had a negatively limiting character that haunted the Director and his faculty for many years. The purpose of The Cambridge School, as stated in the catalog, emphasized "domestic architecture" and "landscape architecture with particular reference to domestic work." Another statement in the catalog read: "It is realized that domestic [architecture] and landscape architecture have come to be distinct branches of the professions, which require special training, but are better practiced on a foundation of general architectural knowledge." Within a very short time, Mr. Frost was convinced that domestic design in either field was not a distinct and separate branch but was indeed an integral part of each profession. The curriculum changed gradually to include the full range of both professions, but the public impression that the School was limited to training women to design small houses and gardens persisted doggedly for many years.

In 1943, Mr. Frost spoke of the prevailing attitude of those early years as one in which "the average architect was more concerned with domestic design than with the creation of great commercial, transportation, or governmental buildings for the very good reason that thousands of houses must be built to one school, hospital, bank, city hall, or courthouse. The American public...was appreciative... of good houses." He described the collaboration of Mr. Pond and himself as:

> "an early example, perhaps the first in any school, of an architect and a landscape architect thrown together on an equal footing and required to teach together the same group of students with varying aims. Had we been more experienced in our separate fields the results might have been different....One of us, the architect, was concerned with buildings, their design, construction, and mechanical equipment; the other, the landscape architect, was concerned with ground areas, their design and construction for human use, their relation to and their control of structures....[We] accepted the principle that design... was inclusive, that one could not create good volumes, nor indeed practical ones, without an appreciation of areas and of the spatial relationship of the volume to its surroundings; that the building *and* its surroundings comprised the design, rather than the building *or* its surroundings."

Although not mentioned specifically, good scale was everlastingly a primary concern of these two men — the scale of the elements themselves, the scale of the detail, and the related scale of the comprehensive design. Probably because the emphasis at that time was on domestic design, they were greatly concerned with the human scale, the suitability of the designed areas and volumes to the people using them. They deplored the almost total lack of common concept between the two professional schools at Harvard. Knowing that their views would have little impact on the traditional systems of which they were but a minor part, they used "The Little School" as an escape. There they felt free to do as they pleased. Of their general attitude, Mr. Frost wrote:

> "We were making our own traditions. Our past was all in the future, an enviable condition....And so we criticized — our students, our elders, the great and the near great in history, and each other — often to the audible amusement of our students. It was an undignified procedure according to all the tenets of education and as such would have been carefully avoided within the halls of the University, except perhaps in our own offices behind closed doors."

22

World War I

All who remember the early days of The Cambridge School agree that aside from the usual drafting room chatter related to the work in hand the chief topic of conversation was World War I, not thought of then in capital letters with a Roman numeral but simply as "the war." In 1915, most Americans were aware of events in Europe, but they seemed very remote; in 1916, it was obvious to the students and faculty, as it was to many others, that the United States was rapidly drifting toward war; and after war was declared in April 1917, it was uppermost in the minds of all. The small faculty of The Cambridge School was affected disproportionately. Both Bremer Pond and Martin Mowrer joined the Quartermaster Corps. Abby Christensen left for Europe to serve in the Y.M.C.A. Hut at Nancy. Henry Frost not only took on the full responsibility of running the infant school, as well as his teaching assignments at Harvard, but also worked with the United States Housing Corporation of the Department of Labor. Professor Pray was busy laying out training camps for the Quartermaster Corps. Professor Warren's death on November 21, 1917, was attributed in part to overexertion in war work. The small but growing professional school for women thus lost an inspiring friend.[4]

The First Graduates

Interpretation of the few official records of the early years, as well as later references to that period, vary from one researcher to another, and now even the women who were there at the time tend to be hazy about events and dates. It is known, however, that in March 1919 the School circulated an announcement that read: "The Cambridge School of Domestic Architecture and Landscape Architecture announces that it will admit twelve new students for the academic year 1919-20." This may have been the first time that the slightly changed official name of the School was used. In several later publications the title above is followed by a note to the reader: "Usually called 'The Cambridge School'."

As the School had no authority to grant academic degrees, the students then and for many years afterward were awarded certificates upon satisfactory completion of the three-year course of study. Katherine Brooks and Rose Greely were the first to receive such certificates, in 1919. By June 1920, eleven students had finished the required courses and presumably had been awarded certificates. Of these eleven women, the five landscape architects were Katherine Brooks Norcross, Rose Greely, Mary P. Cunningham, Elizabeth D. Jones, and Henrietta Marquis Pope. Since Abby Christensen was not included, it is most likely that she went off to France without completing all requirements. The six architects in this early group were Eleanor Raymond, Gertrude Sawyer, Laura Cox, Esther L. Kilton,

Ethel B. Power, and Constance Smith Joslin. On balance, this almost equal mixture of the two professions prevailed through the life of The Cambridge School, though at times the scales tilted sharply — first one way and then the other.

---

[1]Although the first students in this course, Gertrude Sawyer and Henrietta Marquis Pope, were officially enrolled at The Cambridge School, their classes usually were held in Professor Pray's office in Robinson Hall or, occasionally, in his home library.

[2]Professor Warren's lectures began at 5:30 and lasted through 7:30. Mr. Frost once said that the students would gladly have stayed another hour, that no one thought of dinner (least of all Professor Warren), but that on those evenings he himself was not welcomed very enthusiastically when he finally got home.

[3]Author's note to reader: If you were awake while reading the first few pages of this history, you will remember that Harvard did NOT accept her. If it had, you would most likely not be reading this story today.

[4]Herbert Langford Warren had been born in England and was educated there and in Germany. His mother was English, but his father was of New England stock, and when young Langford was nineteen he was sent to study at the Massachusetts Institute of Technology. Later he worked for H. H. Richardson and in partnership with various other architects until he went to teach at Harvard in 1893. He became the first dean of the Faculty of Architecture. Being unusually familiar with and keenly interested in the architectural monuments of Europe, he was deeply affected by the widespread devastation of the war. He dreamed of the day when he could go back to help in reconstruction work. He wrote, lectured, and met with groups that were anxious to send help from the United States, but all these activities were far beyond his rather limited physical strength, so his personal dreams could not be realized.

Figure 2.1 — The building to the left is No. 4 Brattle Street as it looked shortly after World War I. On Valentine's Day 1916, a few women arrived here to study in the offices of Henry A. Frost, architect, and Bremer W. Pond, landscape architect. This educational experiment, first called only "the little school," eventually became the Smith College Graduate School of Architecture and Landscape Architecture in Cambridge, known as The Cambridge School. Although it moved to different quarters several times, the school was always located near Harvard Square.

Figure 2.2 — Professor James Sturgis Pray, city planner, whose faith in women's ability to learn and practice a profession encouraged teachers and students alike. Professor Pray was President of the American Society of Landscape Architects from 1915 to 1918.

Figure 2.3 — Professor Bremer Whidden Pond, landscape architect, the other half of the faculty in the office school that flippant Harvard students sometimes called the "Frost and Pond Day Nursery."

Figure 2.4 — Katherine Brooks (Norcross), whose desire to study at Harvard in 1915 accidentally brought about the experiment in the nameless school that later became The Cambridge School.

Figure 2.5 — Rose Greely, one of the first group of students in the little school that had no name. Later, Rose Greely practiced landscape architecture in Washington, D.C., and in 1936 was the first Cambridge School graduate to be elected an ASLA Fellow. Of the twenty-eight women elected as Fellows by 1978, ten were from The Cambridge School.

Figure 2.6 — Abby Christensen, one of the first students in the office school and the first teaching assistant in the drafting room. The photo was taken at her home in Beaufort, South Carolina, where she practiced for many years after returning from World War I service in France.

Figure 2.7 — A first-year Cambridge School student measuring a small summer cottage in 1918. Throughout the life of the school, all students were required to measure actual buildings and outdoor spaces in detail.

Figure 2.8 — Mildred Rutherford and Gertrude Olds (Schupp), students at The Cambridge School in the early days, waiting for a bus after a short vacation away from their studies.

3

The Formative Years

During the early 1920's the number of students seeking admission to The Cambridge School continued to increase, while four women — Theodora Kimball, Mary P. Cunningham, Mary Nearing, and Frances Jackson — were added to the Instructing Staff. All but Theodora Kimball, who at that time was librarian of the School of Landscape Architecture at Harvard and a prolific writer of articles on the profession, were recent graduates of The Cambridge School. Space was still a problem. The young ladies were constantly outgrowing their quarters, and small annexes had been established at 1278 Massachusetts Avenue and in the Abbott Building on Harvard Square. At 1278 Massachusetts Avenue, an ice cream parlor on the floor below served unforgettable coffee ice cream sundaes with hot chocolate sauce. In more businesslike terms the official Bulletin issued in May 1919 says reassuringly that "the rooms are well lighted, clean, with modern conveniences. The students have draughting tables similar to those used in the offices. The equipment in the way of books, magazines and plates is good and is being added to constantly." Perhaps the additions were made too constantly, for in 1921 the entire school was moved into larger quarters at 13 Boyleston Street. The official name of the school, which had changed slightly every once in a while, retained the 1919 version — The Cambridge School of Domestic Architecture and Landscape Architecture — but about this time the cumbersome and somewhat coy phrase "usually called The Cambridge School" was dropped from official stationery. Like the first two years of the School's existence, the decade of the 1920's was a remarkably innovative period for The Cambridge School.

The Landscape Exchange Problems

The fact that the school itself seemed to be booming did not mean

33

that women had become universally recognized in their professions. Their future was discussed, however, at the Third National Conference of Instruction on Landscape Architecture, held at Cornell in June 1922. The Committee on Education respectfully reported its approval of training women in landscape architecture, preferably in coeducational schools.[1] It added that "the study of stenography would be especially useful to women in helping them work in an office." Not stated but implicit was the thought that it might also be even more useful to the men in charge. The blow was somewhat softened, however, by the last paragraph of the report, which read: "Opposition to the training of women in landscape work has been offered by some on the grounds that a woman may not use such training in practice throughout her life. The same might apply to many men who take up the work."

At the Fifth National Conference, at the University of Michigan in 1924, an intercollegiate program of Landscape Exchange Problems was suggested and was acted on almost immediately. The aim of such a program was to provide regular channels through which the work of students of landscape architecture in several schools could be compared on a competitive basis. It was an attempt to break away occasionally from the somewhat limited practice of professors in any one school devising problems for their own students and having the solutions judged by a presumably impartial jury that might indeed include professors from the same school. In the proposed intercollegiate program, the problems were to be devised by a group of professors from different schools, then simultaneously announced by the head of each school, and supervised by one of its professors of landscape design. On meeting all requirements, including a stringent deadline, the solutions were to be sent on a rotating basis to one of the participating schools to be judged by an impartial jury and then circulated among all the schools that had entered the competition. Such a comparative program was expected to help establish standards of training in landscape architecture. Obviously, it was also meant to encourage hard work and to bring out the best in both students and faculties.

The program took on actual substance when E. Gorton Davis of Cornell arranged the first Exchange Problem. Although for many years landscape architects from many institutions worked hard on this ambitious program, which continued into the 1970's, the most ardent supporter and prime mover who kept it alive and vigorous was Stanley White of the University of Illinois. During the summer of 1924 he and William Richard Sears of Ohio State University established the basic organization and administrative procedures and succeeded in getting all the mechanics in working order for the academic year 1924-25. The original group of landscape schools accepting the challenge of the new program were The Cambridge School, Cornell University, Harvard University, Iowa State College, John Huntington Institute (Cleveland), The Lowthorpe School, Missouri Botanical Gardens, New York Chapter (ASLA) Atelier, Ohio State University, University of Illinois, University of Michigan, and University of Minnesota. Not all institutions active in the Landscape Exchange Problems program entered the competition every year nor did those who entered always submit solutions to all problems. The percentage of entries remained high, however, and the undertaking in which competition was very keen was considered to be a good training device, though the exhibiting and judging of the students' work was a time-consuming and at times an exhausting process.

Outstanding landscape architects practicing at the time were chosen as jurors, with Ferrucio Vitale, Bryant Fleming, Percival Gallagher, A. D. Taylor, and O. C. Simonds serving as the first jury. Eliza Birnie of The Cambridge School received one of the awards of the first competition, and in the following years, Cambridge School students regularly won a high percentage of Exchange Problem honors.[2]

The Cambridge School, Inc.

The fall of 1924 was significant for The Cambridge School. On October 1st the first meeting of the Board of Trustees of The Cambridge School, Inc. (note the new name) was held at 13 Boyleston Street. Present at the meeting, aside from Mr. Frost, were Bremer Pond, Secretary, Professor G. H. Edgell, John Nolen, H. F. Ramhofer, and Ethel Power, who had received her Certificate in Architecture from The Cambridge School in 1920. Mentioned in the Minutes as Trustees but not present at this first meeting were: Byron S. Hurlbut, William Emerson, and James S. Pray. Part of the business conducted dealt with the election of Henry Atherton Frost as the Director for the newly incorporated school. The existing faculty, heretofore called the Instructing Staff, was approved for the year 1924-25. The "By-Laws of The Cambridge School, Incorporated, as approved by the incorporators..." were discussed at some length. Mr. Frost, now officially the Director, named Bremer Pond and Henry Ramhofer to serve with him as an Executive Committee. The Minutes indicate that most of the discussion at this rather long meeting was about the things that all business meetings must dwell on over and over again, finances. As always, the School was operating on a very tight budget, and the Trustees discussed various ways of raising money for running expenses and scholarships. Gifts in fairly large amounts were coming in from the alumnae as well as other friends of the School, but they were never enough to provide a comfortable margin. Finally, two interesting, though tentative, matters came up for discussion: 1) whether to publicize The Cambridge School widely through magazine advertisements and, possibly, through exhibitions of students' work, and 2) whether to establish a course in Interior Decorating. (Courses in Town Planning and Urban Housing had been added to the curriculum in 1918-19 and were first taught by Professor Pray and Herbert W. Blaney.)

The Director favored both suggestions. He had always thought that the detailed design of the inside of a house, a design planned to suit the occupants' taste and living habits, was as important as the structural design. How best to inform potential students about The Cambridge School was another matter. In speaking of the scatter approach to publicity while he was reminiscing in 1943, Mr. Frost wondered whether the School's first "entirely shameless and self-conscious effort at popular appeal," the May 1916 announcement printed on sage-green deckle-edged paper with a "natty" envelope to match, had really influenced any of the students who came to "The Little School" that fall. He commented that "the trouble with advertising is that you never know whether it did or whether it didn't. I remember many years later we put on an intensive campaign of 'public information'.... I visited...schools and colleges, gave talks, held seminars, put up exhaustive and exhausting exhibitions. The next year we had the largest registration of entering students in our career, but not one...came from any of the institutions I had visited. Think what the registration might have been had I sat quietly at home by my fireside all through those cold winter months." Apparently at the time of the meeting in 1924, he thought widespread advertising worth a try. The Board, however, wanted to think about both proposals a little longer.

The Cambridge School, Inc., established as an entity in October 1924, was short-lived, operating under that name for only a month. We learn from a brief history of the School, probably written by Mr. Frost in the late 1920's, that "in November, 1924, the School was incorporated under the laws of Massachusetts as...The Cambridge School of Domestic Architecture and Landscape Architecture." Later, the word "Domestic" was seriously questioned by Mr. Frost, as giving a false impression of the training offered, but it was not dropped officially until 1932.

Many Problems and Solution to One

Aside from the perennial lack of funds, which always held first place among the problems of the School, the need to grant academic degrees instead of, or as well as, certificates was becoming more and more urgent by the mid-1920's. The lack of a recognized degree proved more of a stumbling block to the architects in the competitive professional world than to the landscape architects, and this was reflected in a temporary decrease in the number of architectural students. In 1924, during one such period of imbalance in the registration, a small mutinous protest (surely a very polite one) developed among the landscape students. Although Bremer Pond had returned from the war and was included in the faculty list of 1920-21, his responsibilities at the Harvard School of Landscape Architecture, and after 1922 as Secretary of the ASLA, demanded most of his time. He remained on the Board of Trustees of The Cambridge School throughout its existence, but he did not teach there full time after 1921. The landscape students pointed out that although they outnumbered the architectural students, they had no continuous leadership among the faculty but instead had to depend almost entirely upon intermittent lectures and critiques given by visiting instructors. Though fewer in number, the architectural students could learn from several architects on the permanent faculty. In a report written several years later, Mr. Frost referred to the 1924 protest and said that he had been searching for "the best available man in the country" to teach landscape design and added that the students did not understand how difficult it was to find good landscape instructors. His search finally ended in October 1926 with the appointment of William Richard Sears to The Cambridge School faculty.

Mr. Sears, more widely known as "Dick," was certainly well qualified for the job. He had been graduated from the Harvard School of Landscape Architecture in 1920 and then taught a year at Iowa State College before studying abroad as the recipient of the Charles Eliot Travelling Fellowship. After returning from Europe he worked a year for Olmsted Brothers in Brookline and then went to Ohio State University as Resident Professor of Landscape Architecture. He was very successful in building up the Department of Landscape Architecture at Ohio, and he was active in the sometimes tedious work of the Landscape Exchange Problems program. Mr. Frost had known him for some years, and he was pleased with himself for having persuaded Dick Sears to join the small school in Cambridge that had passed the early experimental days but was still not widely recognized in the professional world.

Field Studies Abroad and At Home

In 1927 the first three-month travel and study course, sponsored jointly by The Cambridge School and The Lowthorpe School, was conducted through England, France, and Italy by Mr. Frost and Mr. Sears. In 1928 an eight-week summer course was held at Oxford University, preceded by a three-week trip through England. (A bit of retaliatory discrimination seems to have entered here, as at a January 1928 meeting the Trustees of The Cambridge School voted that "...men should not be admitted to the Summer School at Oxford." However, even Trustees sometimes change their minds, and a list of members of the 1928 Summer School at Oxford, issued later that year, includes the names of two Harvard men along with the thirteen women who attended.) An ambitious plan for an international summer school — to be held at Cambridge University, England, in 1929, but rotating to other participating institutions after that —unfortunately fell through. The institutions that tried to develop the plan were the School of Architecture at the University of Cambridge; the School of Architecture at the University of Liverpool, the Schools of Architecture and Landscape Architecture at Harvard University; and The Cambridge School. Lowthorpe had dropped out of the foreign travel program after the 1927 trip, but The Cambridge School study and travel trips continued and were considered very worthwhile, truly memorable, by all who went along.[3]

Only a fortunate few could afford the summer courses abroad, but the School arranged many field trips, usually to large estates and small gardens near New York, Philadelphia, Boston, and other smaller centers, mainly in New England. In this way, the students could see construction in various stages of completion as well as the finished work of some of the foremost architects and landscape architects of that period. A visit to Fairsted, the Olmsted office in Brookline, was a yearly event. At least one visitor remembers marveling that so many logical and well-coordinated landscape plans could have issued from that office, which seemed to be a strange mixture of living areas, working space, and storage cubbyholes. The students were too young, perhaps, to know then that for the elder Frederick Law Olmsted personal domestic life and professional life were truly inseparable. The hodgepodge accumulation of material possessions, both personal and professional, as well as the family traditions, had been handed down to the younger generations in the firm that was then called Olmsted Brothers.

Like most professional schools, The Cambridge School encouraged its students to acquire a broad background and called attention to the many cultural advantages of the Boston area but allowed virtually no spare time between required courses for work outside the curriculum. An individual approach and lots of personal initiative were strongly recommended, and when all turned out well, highly commended. But the students found that they were spending all of the day and much of the night in the drafting room working on assigned design problems, and they had little time left for unguided sorties among the treasures of the town.

In relation to all courses and problems, the Director advised the students to "learn to see." By this he meant that they should become more aware of their surroundings than the average person would be and should visualize internal structure as well as seeing outward form, color, and detail. He believed that this ability came only through training the eye. Classes in charcoal drawing, pencil sketching, and water color were scheduled and, through special arrangement, were held at one of several Harvard museums, the Boston Museum of Fine Arts, or other museums in the area. Cambridge itself provided many fine subjects for outdoor sketching. The aim of all such work was twofold — to teach the students to observe carefully and to make them more proficient in rendering their designs so that others could visualize and understand them. All students studied plants, as design elements, at Harvard's Arnold Arboretum in Jamaica Plain and at its Botanic Gardens, first in Cambridge (Gray Gardens) and later in Lexington. The landscape students particularly were expected to learn their plant materials, really learn as much as possible about each plant, not just to identify an oak tree by its leaf.

As the student body changed, so did the faculty. Several generations of students will undoubtedly remember with gratitude and affection their water color classes, indoors and out, with Mary Gay, the amusing and indomitable Miss Gay.[4] Others will remember the endless patience of Frank Rines, who taught them how to see as well as draw. Still others may remember more vividly the rigorous plant hunting hikes over hill and dale, in all kinds of weather, led by Stephen Hamblin, Mary P. Cunningham, or Edith Cochran. The last two had gone through the drill themselves as Cambridge School students, and they did not spare their followers.

Cambridge-Lowthorpe Collaboration

The dissatisfaction expressed earlier by some of the landscape students, before Dick Sears joined the faculty full time, bothered the Director more than he cared to admit. The landscape students had thought that the School's approach to their profession was too strongly architectural. Conversely, the graduates who were out in the field practicing landscape architecture were urging the School to provide even more architectural training. Whether this dichotomous attitude in any way influenced various suggestions that The Cambridge School and The Lowthorpe School should be combined is hard to say. It was argued that Cambridge landscape students might benefit from the plant-oriented training at Lowthorpe and that the Lowthorpe students might benefit just as much from the more intensive architectural training at Cambridge. Whatever the impetus, an informal collaboration between The Cambridge School and The Lowthorpe School was set up on a trial basis during the 1925-26 academic year. It was not much more than an exchange of students for a term at a time. The two schools were on friendly terms, and some of the same instructors taught at both, but it was difficult to combine them very solidly because of the difference in their locations, physical and financial assets, teaching goals, and general backgrounds. Lowthorpe was much the older school, and perhaps it was more strongly tied to its own traditions. The collaboration came to an end shortly after the co-sponsored travel study course abroad in 1927, when Lowthorpe began negotiations for an affiliation with Simmons College, an advantageous connection that, if all went well, would require no adjustment to the physical plant in Groton and that could provide academic degrees for its students.

The year 1928 was a fairly crucial one for the future of The Cambridge School and a very busy one for its Director. Along with the usual heavy load of teaching and administrative chores, he was involved with the details of the Summer School at Oxford, as well as a proposal for wider publicity for his own school in Cambridge. He also spent many long hours considering possible solutions to the problem of advanced degrees, and, like the replaying of an old record, the worrisome realization that the School was once more outgrowing its quarters.

Report on Women in Architecture and Landscape Architecture, 1928

As if he hadn't enough to keep him busy, early in 1928 Henry Atherton Frost collaborated with William Richard Sears on a study of *Women in Architecture and Landscape Architecture,* published in June 1928 by the Institute for the Co-ordination of Women's Interests. As this study was rather widely distributed and has been referred to in professional circles from time to time, it seems in order to say a word about the Institute itself. It was financed by the Laura Spelman Rockefeller Memorial and at that time was directed by Ethel Puffer Howes, who with six research assistants and a small staff worked at Smith College for three years, 1925-28. They were concerned about the number of women whose professional careers all too often ended when they married, despite genuine interest and good training at considerable expense. The Institute's aim was to survey the professional world and to pinpoint for women those professions which, they thought, could be interrupted for a few months or years and be resumed later with no great loss to either part of a dual career. The yardstick example they used in surveying many different fields was free-lance writing. That they also chose architecture and landscape architecture as professions that could be dropped temporarily and picked up with ease seems indicative of the fact that at that time almost all women who were trained in those two professions went into private practice after a short apprenticeship in some established professional office. Presumably, these women had the final say about scheduling their time and their careers. Some may have disagreed with this premise.

It is not surprising that an Institute associated with Smith College, even briefly, should make a survey of architecture and landscape architecture, as the College had struggled to maintain an orderly environment from the time it was founded in 1875. In 1928, President Neilson was particularly interested in the opportunities for women in both fields. In their contribution to the Institute's general survey, Frost and Sears were writing for and about women throughout the country, but their advice was, quite naturally, very similar to that which they had been giving The Cambridge School students and alumnae for some time. The theme was invariably thorough training and hard work. Although their comments were generally encouraging, they warned women considering a professional career in architecture or landscape architecture that they might encounter some discrimination among the more conservative schools. They noted the fact that fellowships and scholarships were more likely to be awarded to men than to women and that coeducational schools seemed to have more trouble finding positions for women than for men. Schools exclusively for women, they added, had no difficulty placing their graduates — not an entirely disinterested and objective comment!

A few statements in the long report seem somewhat anachronistic, even for the period in which they were written. One such was that women were naturally inclined toward and particularly well suited to work on small residential or domestic jobs, a belief rather widespread at the time but one not necessarily held by the authors. With ever helpful hindsight, some contemporary critics point to this statement as one that by implication relegated women to domestic jobs only, thus fortifying the concept that a woman's place was in the home. At the time the report was written, Henry Frost was convinced that women did better work than men in the residential field, partly because he felt that they had a flair for design related to the human scale and partly because they paid more attention to detail. He did not mean to imply, however, that because they were better than men in one field they were incapable of competing with them in others. Richard Sears probably held the same or similar views. Even while contributing to this report the Director of The Cambridge School was urging his faculty to assume a much broader approach and to assign larger-scale problems. In 1928 the field of residential work was wide open, in fact booming. Throughout the country, large estates with many buildings and ample gardens were in various stages of execution or were simply waiting to be designed. Most, though not all, of the training at The Cambridge School in 1928 was focused on residential work. The men most responsible for this training may be forgiven if they, like many potential clients, failed to foresee the Market Crash of 1929 and its widespread effects.

Toward the end of the report the authors posed a number of questions and answered one of them — "Should women be advised to enter these professions?" — with the flat statement: "The question of success in either architecture or landscape architecture does not necessarily involve sex." They went on to say that neither men nor women should enter either profession unless they were willing to undertake serious training and withstand inevitable knocks and rebuffs. In their view, if a reasonably intelligent woman persisted in spite of discouragement, hard work, and necessary sacrifices, she had a reasonable opportunity for success in congenial work.

New Quarters

Encouraging words about the professions and the merits of sound training notwithstanding, the inability to grant academic degrees hung over The Cambridge School like the sword of Damocles. Moreover, the young ladies, true to form, were once more feeling crowded. The increased number of students and the courses that were expanded to take care of them demanded more space. At this critical point, the School acquired its final and completely adequate home through the generosity of one of its recent graduates. In 1928, Faith Bemis (Mrs. John Gaw Meem) bought the fine old Dalby House and ample lot that had been the headquarters of the Cantabrigia Club at 53 Church Street, near Harvard Square, and leased the building to the School at a very low rent. Available records become hazy at this point, but with further outside financial help it was possible to add to the Dalby House a north-lighted wing that contained two large drafting rooms, accommodating a total of sixty students and their large drafting tables with a little elbow room to spare — a far cry from the oriental rugs and card tables in the Brooks' home, where it had all started barely thirteen years before!

---

[1] That this conference favored coeducational schools is surprising, since the First Conference was organized at Harvard, probably under the guidance of its chairman, James Sturgis Pray, and Bremer Pond, and delegates from both Lowthorpe and The Cambridge School attended.

[2] Anyone interested in the Landscape Exchange Problems in detail will find much more information in the ASLA Quarterly, *Landscape Architecture,* from January 1925 through October 1942; in *Landscape Architectural Education* by Gary O. Robinette, published by Kendall/Hunt Publishing Company, Dubuque, Iowa, 1973; and in *The Teaching of Landscape Architecture,* by Stanley White, published privately by Samuel Peaslee Snow, Auburn, Alabama, 1953.

[3] Author's note: While doing research for this study, I received many letters and comments from former Cambridge School students. They show that even now those who went on one or more foreign study trips are unanimous in their high praise of the plan and grateful for having had such a rewarding experience. The Hurlbut Scholarship, established by Mrs. Hurlbut in memory of her husband, Harvard Professor Byron S. Hurlbut, who was on the Board of Trustees of The Cambridge School until his death in 1930, made it possible for me to join the 1931 study trip to England, led by Mr. Frost. Like many of my colleagues, I am forever appreciative of the experiences of that English summer, dismally cold and rainy though it was. My wardrobe consisted of two 3-piece suits, one heavy cotton knit for rough wear, the other a silk knit for dress. As we were allowed to take only one smallish suitcase, I saved precious space by wearing both outfits at the same time all summer. When occasion demanded, a quick reversal from inside to

outside in the nearest Ladies Room upheld the necessary decorum and at the same time kept me from freezing to death. Thus warmly dressed, I was able to concentrate on my surroundings instead of my goose pimples and learn something about the English countryside and gardens. As the days went by, suitcase space became more and more of a problem for everyone, and an odd assortment of string bags and incongruous objects (including a military dress sword picked up at an antique shop) seemed to spring from every appendage of automobile and person. Nevertheless, the camera, sketch pad, notebook, and six-foot rule required of each of us were never jettisoned.

[4]Miss Gay died in Duxbury, Massachusetts, in the fall of 1977, aged 103. She and her late sister, Mrs. Charles Bittinger had been friends of the Alcott family in Concord. Mrs. Bittinger once told the author of how she and Mary dressed up in their best white frocks, hats, and gloves and without parental guidance paid a respectful call on the venerable Ralph Waldo Emerson, who received the little girls most graciously.

Figure 3.1 — Henry A. Frost, Director of The Cambridge School, and friend.

Figure 3.2 — William Richard Sears, who from 1926 to 1932 greatly improved the training in landscape architecture at The Cambridge School.

Figure 3.3 — The Lowthorpe School of Landscape Architecture in Groton, Massachusetts. Lowthorpe formally collaborated briefly with The Cambridge School in the late 1920's. Informally the two schools exchanged views on teaching landscape architecture during many years of neighborly association.

Figure 3.4 — Lowthorpe students on a garden trip to estates in the Berkshires in 1935.

Figure 3.5 — In 1928, The Cambridge School acquired a new home at 53 Church Street. The school remained at this address until it was closed in 1942.

Figure 3.6 — The Cambridge School in winter.

Figure 3.7 — The Director in London, loading baggage while on a Cambridge School study trip to England in the late 1920's.

Figure 3.8 — Henry A. Frost and students in England in 1931.

Figure 3.9 — The Cambridge School study group having tea at the Trout Inn near Oxford in 1931.

Figure 3.10 — Elizabeth Abbott (Fries) and Florence Smith acting as scale figures at a doorway in Kent, 1931.

Figure 3.11 — Measuring architectural details in an English garden. Though measuring and sketching were required on all study trips, these students seem to approach the task a bit gingerly.

Figure 3.12 — Maud Sargent and Dorothy May Anderson examining transportation possibilities in Paris while on a short vacation from study in England in 1931.

4

The Dilemma

As the 1920's drew to a close, many of the problems of the early years had been solved. An excellent faculty and good students were keeping scholastic achievements at top notch, adequate working space was finally available for all, and money, so badly needed, was beginning to come in in fairly large amounts. Unresolved, however, was the dilemma of advanced degrees. A professional degree had become a legal requirement for practicing architecture in most states. Clearly, the handwriting was on the wall for landscape architecture as well. Excellent as its training record was, The Cambridge School had neither the large enrollment nor the financial endowment required to qualify as a chartered independent graduate school empowered to grant academic degrees. Of the many possibilities examined by the Director and the Trustees as a solution, an alliance with some recognized institution that could grant degrees of Master of Architecture (M.Arch.) and Master of Landscape Architecture (M.L.A.) seemed the best. The question was: Which institution?

Possible Partners

Looking back from the 1970's, it seems that some of the most obvious solutions were overlooked. Not so. Although most of the faculty members of The Cambridge School were also on the faculty of the Harvard Schools of Architecture and Landscape Architecture, and the routinely changing Board of Trustees of The Cambridge School was heavily weighted with Harvard men, Harvard University in the late 1920's had no more idea of admitting women than it had when Professor Pray was forced to turn away Katherine Brooks. (It is interesting, if not ironic, to note that about this time The Cambridge School was considering admitting men.) At least one advisor thought that if The Cambridge School were entirely staffed by Harvard professors, though at the time only two or three faculty members were not from Harvard, President Lowell might change his mind. Others, perhaps those who knew him better, said it would make no difference at all. The desirability of Harvard advanced degrees for Cambridge School graduates was often discussed, but pursuing this remote possibility would have been entirely unrealistic. Also, Mr. Frost was somewhat fearful that in any closer connection between the two schools doing comparable work, Harvard might impose restrictions on the more personal approach to teaching at The Cambridge School.

From the point of view of sex, location, and academic prestige, Radcliffe College, closely tied to Harvard, seemed to be the most logical choice for an affiliation, and it was preferred by most of the Trustees throughout all pertinent discussions. Miss Ada Louise Comstock was President of Radcliffe at that time; she was enthusiastic about the work she observed at The Cambridge School and sympathetic with it because of the scholastic problems it faced. For Radcliffe to grant M.Arch. and M.L.A. degrees, however, Miss Comstock would have had to go before the Massachusetts Legislature and plead her case for a change in the college charter without the approval of Harvard's President Lowell. This she was unwilling to do.

Although it held out little hope as a solution to The Cambridge School's dilemma, a suggestion made by Miss Comstock and supported by Mr. Frost probably would be more feasible today than it was in the late 1920's. She proposed establishing a Graduate School of Architecture and Landscape Architecture serving "the seven outstanding women's colleges of the east." Undergraduate programs were to be expanded, or established if they were not already underway. Upon completion of the work of the proposed graduate school a student would receive an advanced degree from "the college of her choice." A four-part outline of "Tentative suggestions for a Graduate School of Architecture and Landscape Architecture controlled by a group of Women's Colleges" was considered at a meeting of college presidents early in 1928. But even simplified to the four basic matters of 1) present conditions, 2) general governing board, 3) financial control, and 4) granting of advanced academic degrees, the tentative plan obviously held all the seeds of an administrative nightmare. Imaginative and progressive though it was, it died quietly.

As they had done many times before, the enthusiastic supporters of a Cambridge-Lowthorpe combination once again pointed out the advantages of such an alliance and the dissuaders called attention to its disadvantages, but it would have been a meaningless solution for both schools. Lowthorpe could no more grant degrees on its own than could The Cambridge School, and during the discussions of 1928 Lowthorpe became an affiliate of Simmons College to accomplish this end.[1]

About this time, Columbia University contemplated establishing a School of Landscape Architecture in connection with its School of Architecture. The advantages of New York as a more central urban location than the Boston area were brought up before The Cambridge School Board of Trustees, but apparently they were rejected after very little discussion.[2]

Evidently no consideration was given to the Massachusetts Institute of Technology (M.I.T.) which had an active Department of Architecture but which had given up its Department of Landscape Architecture in 1900. Simmons College was very briefly suggested and rejected, probably on the grounds that the disciplines offered were not compatible with the goals of The Cambridge School. There is no indication that Wellesley, a women's college conveniently located in the area, might have been considered.

Although in terms of locational convenience Smith College was remote from Cambridge, many favorable aspects brought it quite naturally into the discussion of possible affiliations. The President of Smith College at that time was William Allan Neilson, who had a keen personal interest in both architecture and landscape architecture as well as the broad range of interests in literature and other scholarly matters for which he was well known. He was aware of The Cambridge School from its very beginning, having been a member of the Harvard faculty before going to Smith in 1917, and he was an unswervingly staunch supporter of its aims and policies. He and Mr. Frost held very similar views on the education of women and had been exploring ways of forming a connection between their two institutions since early 1926. Gradually during the 1920's, Mr. Frost had come to believe that women received better training when taught separately from men, and partly for this reason he favored affiliation with a women's college. In the eventful year 1928, Mr. Neilson met twice with the Board of Trustees of The Cambridge School, in June and in October, to discuss tentative proposals.

Background on Smith College

Reasons other than personal friendship and professional respect between two men influenced the ultimate decision to affiliate The Cambridge School with Smith College. Some background on the College itself may help clarify the logic of a Smith connection. In 1875 the fourteen young women who arrived in Northampton to study at the new college, made possible by Sophia Smith, were interested in Latin, Greek, Chemistry, and Medicine. The range of interests and offerings soon widened considerably, and early in its history Smith College developed and has always maintained a keen, and for the most part enlightened, interest in the landscape setting of its buildings.[3]

Laurenus Clark Seelye, Smith's first president, envisaged the campus as a botanic garden that would have aesthetic as well as scientific value. He first hired Bowditch & Copeland to plan the grounds around the few earliest buildings, but apparently little was accomplished and no plans of their work were kept. In 1890 he called in the landscape architecture firm of Olmsted, Olmsted and Eliot to lay out the campus, then a mere twenty-seven acres mostly occupied by some dozen buildings placed much too close together to permit development on a grand scale.

In 1894, President Seelye appointed to the faculty a young Harvard professor, Dr. William Francis Ganong, as Professor of Botany and Director of the Botanic Garden. Dr. Ganong kept a keen eye on the botanic garden, but much credit for its success is also due to the work of three outstanding horticulturists — Edward J. Canning, Henry E. Downer, and John Ellis — who spanned many years as Head Gardeners at Smith. All three had been trained at Kew Gardens, England, and they not only supervised the maintenance of the grounds but conducted the laboratory work for classes in horticulture as well. Each in his own way dreamed of a campus that would eventually be internationally known not just for its botanic garden but as a high-ranking arboretum as well, and they planted many rare species of trees. The campus was beautifully sited on a slope above a widening of Mill River known as Paradise Pond, and the botanic garden nearby was always a main focal point. The succession of men in charge implemented the Olmsted plan along with some of their own dreams with remarkable consistency, but in spite of their efforts, as the years went by the "campus plan" came to look very much like a crazy quilt. Development was invariably and inevitably curtailed not by the lay of the land but by land ownership.

Architecture did not fare as well as landscape architecture in the early days at Smith. From the beginning the College bought up residential properties, at foot-frontage prices, here and there as they chanced to come on the market. This piecemeal approach produced a surprising and colorful mixture of "town and gown," as the oddly assorted parcels of land were almost never contiguous, but it had its drawbacks. A few of the buildings that came with the much needed land were beautiful and historically interesting, but many were not well adapted to college life. Despite their locations, the old houses were remodeled a bit and used, while a building program for dormitories marched along ever so slowly. The additional areas purchased were not large enough for a comprehensive group of buildings better suited to their purpose, nor was "big money" available for an adequate building fund.

The original college grounds suffered. Because so much had been spent on bits and pieces of property, little money was left in the buildings and grounds budget for coherent plans, old or new. The campus guardians were understandably envious of their counterparts in other private institutions, like Vassar and Wellesley, whose grounds had been granted to them in large acreages. In time, all three head gardeners left Smith for jobs more to their liking, and by the late 1920's the campus, then approaching 200 acres, was showing the lack of their skilled attention. In 1914, the college had missed an opportunity, possibly not the only one, to gain more coherence in the general layout of the campus, when it disregarded the master plan the Committee on Buildings and Grounds had commissioned John Nolen of Cambridge to present to it. Whether his plan for the existing campus and a proposed extension along Elm Street was not carried out because it seemed a more formal design than the committee had in mind, or whether costs were prohibitive, is not known. The Nolen Plan bears little resemblence to the campus today. A fairly elaborate amphitheater descended the slope to Paradise Pond, complete with a Greek theater on the shore and an island stage across the water. Smith alumnae of classes after 1920 might be surprised to learn that a fairly large athletic field was planned to replace a smaller one on Paradise Road, the site of the Quad Complex today.

On the academic front, Smith offered undergraduate courses related to landscape architecture, beginning in 1900 with a course in Horticulture. This course was concerned primarily with the identification, propagation, and care of plants, but also included studies of their use in ornamental planting. As early as 1914 a course entitled Landscape Architecture was offered by the Botany Department, and it flourished under the strong guidance of Edna B. Stoddard (later Mrs. Ramseyer).[4] In 1919, Kate Ries Koch, a Cornell graduate in landscape architecture, came to Smith from teaching positions at Cornell and Vassar. She was in charge of the undergraduate training in landscape architecture until her retirement from the College in 1952. Through her suggestion and the firm support of President Neilson, the courses in landscape architecture were transferred from the Botany Department to the Art Department in 1928. Though a subtle but recurrent administrative endeavor to tuck landscape architecture back into the Botany Department (on the grounds that it was not truly an art but merely a gardening skill) occasionally created a bit of interdepartmental friction, this move favored a better standing for the College among other institutions teaching the subject.

Architecture, as a comprehensive discipline, lagged behind landscape architecture in the early days at Smith. The history of architecture was included in the history of art courses, but it was not until 1929, when talk of a possible affiliation with The Cambridge School was underway, that Karl Scott Putnam was appointed to the Art Department to teach architectural design, construction, and history. He had been trained at the University of Pennsylvania and Columbia University and had maintained a very active practice in Northampton since 1912. He was well known as a sound designer with impeccable taste. No better person could have been chosen to introduce Smith undergraduates to the exciting world of architecture, which he did until his retirement in 1952.

At the graduate level, a strong link between Smith and The Cambridge School existed long before any talk of affiliation. From the earliest days of The Cambridge School, Smith graduates tended to outnumber students from other institutions. One year, nineteen of some forty students were from Smith. In 1919, while still a student at The Cambridge School, Mary P. Cunningham took on the teaching of landscape architecture at Smith for the short period between the eras of Miss Stoddard and Miss Koch. Ada Louise Comstock, who would have preferred to have The Cambridge School affiliated with Radcliffe, was herself a Smith graduate, had taught at Smith, and had received an honorary degree from her alma mater.[5] She was the College Dean at the time she left Smith in 1923 to become Dean and later President at Radcliffe. During the discussions of the late 1920's and early 1930's she was on the Board of Trustees of Smith College and also on The Cambridge School Council. Thus it seems that the meetings between the President of Smith College and the Board of Trustees of The Cambridge School and its Director came about not just by chance but through a recognition of long-standing mutual interests.

Discussion, Tentative Proposals, and Alternatives

The Trustee's meeting of June 4, 1928, was cordial and productive on most long-range goals, though many details of the proposed affiliation required further study. Mr. Neilson was predisposed to support any plan whereby Smith College could grant advanced degrees to Cambridge School graduates. The consensus of this first meeting was that if an affiliation with Smith proved feasible the School would remain in Cambridge, with the same faculty, and that The Cambridge School, not Smith College, would assume all financial responsibilities. The last condition was Mr. Frost's preference, as he wanted to keep the School the autonomous entity it always had been. Mr. Neilson favored limiting the number of students, and he strongly preferred having the first year of graduate training given at Smith College, in Northampton. He added, however, that such a change need not be carried out immediately or carried out at all if it affected the curriculum of The Cambridge School adversely. It was agreed that in any final plan there was to be no cancellation of The Cambridge School Certificate for those few students who entered without a Bachelor's degree. Once more, the name of the School came up for

58

discussion, and Mr. Neilson said he had no objection to any name chosen so long as it was followed by the phrase "In Affiliation with Smith College."

Although much of the June meeting seems to have been devoted to informal discussion, it was formally voted by the Trustees that "If the proposed merger with Smith or any other institution goes forward, it is understood that the school is to be in Cambridge for at least ten years, and that it shall continue to enjoy any property that it may have in Cambridge at the time the merger is made." The Director was asked to submit a comprehensive report on The Cambridge School. This he did on October 25, 1928.

At this point one is suddenly overtaken by the nostalgic "what if" syndrome of wandering thoughts that dwell on that other path. What if the first year's graduate training had been given in Northampton as Mr. Neilson wanted it to be? Would it have made any difference in the development and final outcome of The Cambridge School? One of the reasons President Davis gave later on for closing the Graduate School in Cambridge was his desire to maintain all elements of Smith College on one campus. As the years went by the official bonds between the undergraduate and graduate schools became stronger, but the personal bonds of loyalty among the faculties, students, and alumnae of the two separated groups were never strongly felt on either side. What if Professor Hurlbut's somewhat prophetic suggestion of June 1928, that the School should wait a while longer before joining any other institution or should set a clear and definite time limit on affiliation, had been considered more seriously? He could see no reason why within the next twenty years The Cambridge School "should not become part of that great institution in Cambridge" and that looking ahead one could see "that a union with Harvard is the natural and wise step to work for." To this suggestion, Professor Edgell — who was then Dean of the Harvard School of Architecture and who had strongly favored a union with Radcliffe — replied that although twenty years was not long in the life of a school, in this case it was too long to wait. He feared that the standards so carefully built up might be sacrificed if the students were not granted degrees soon. One could go on indefinitely with "what if" fantasies. What if there had been no market crash in 1929 and no depression in the 1930's? What if there had been no World War II? What if President Neilson's successor had shared his enthusiasm for promoting the work of The Cambridge School? Would any of the "what ifs" have made a difference in the status of women in the profession of landscape architecture? The careers of women have been influenced by many things other than the quality of their training.

The comprehensive report on The Cambridge School, submitted to the Trustees by the Director in October 1928, is worth considering in some detail. It tells much about the philosophy and policies, as well as the tribulations, of a small professional school for women during the first twelve years or so of its existence. No doubt the writer had in mind not only a progress report for his own Board of Trustees, but also a statement for the enlightenment of the Board of Trustees of some women's college, presumably Smith. The purpose of the School was very simply stated as follows:

1. To provide to graduates of women's colleges, professional training in architecture and in landscape architecture, the standard of which shall be comparable to that offered in the best collegiate schools.

2. To provide this training to mature students lacking a college degree who are able to satisfy the School that they have a preparation which will enable them to profit by such training and to maintain standards of scholarship required.

The method of achieving this stated purpose was through two curricula, one primarily tailored to the fundamentals of architecture, the other to those of landscape architecture. The two curricula were closely intertwined, and the basic courses relating to each profession were required of all students, regardless of major interests. The Director recommended, or perhaps defended, this approach by saying:

"The School endeavors to correct a fault common to professional schools of ignoring, in their training, the necessary interrelation of the two professions....Thus a student of architecture [at The Cambridge School] learns something of the principles of landscape architecture, while a student of landscape architecture gains a knowledge of architectural principles, and both gain a sympathetic understanding of, and respect for, the complexities of both professions. Such an understanding is necessary in the general practice of the two professions and is absolutely essential in the particular branches with which The Cambridge School is chiefly concerned."[6]

The relative enrollment of students in architecture and landscape architecture fluctuated constantly. The entering class one year would be mostly architects, with only a few landscape architects, and the next year it would be reversed, with many more women wanting to become landscape architects than were willing to devote their lives to architecture. When asked by an alumna why this happened, Mr. Frost answered that only Henrietta Cantabrigia knew the true answer and she wasn't telling.[7] In 1928 the enrollment of architectural students had been decreasing markedly, while the number of landscape students had steadily increased. The Director attributed this imbalance chiefly to a growing need for an advanced degree to practice architecture, whereas a similar need was not yet felt as keenly in the field of landscape architecture. He commented on the situation as follows:

"For several years after its foundation in 1916, the tendency of the School was strongly architectural....At that time the collegiate schools of architecture were glad to advise women to attend a school such as ours....[About the mid-1920's] a change in attitude of certain of the collegiate schools of architecture was noticeable. They were beginning to welcome women. It was natural that [the architectural students] should turn to....the collegiate architectural schools, with their greater financial resources enabling them to employ design instructors beyond our power at present to emulate, and their ability to grant professional degrees which have become generally necessary to the practice of architecture in most states. The long establishment of many architectural schools has given them a national reputation. In addition to this, women students sometimes feel that men are naturally better than they are in professional work, and that, therefore, they will get better results from their efforts if they are in a school composed largely of men students who can serve as pace makers. It should also be remembered that the number of women in architectural schools throughout the country is much smaller than in landscape schools. Women turn more naturally to landscape work."

Whether the last statement was true then or is now is beside the point. Mr. Frost thought that the preponderance of landscape students in 1928 was due in part to the addition of William Richard Sears, widely known and respected in the field of landscape architecture, to The Cambridge School faculty. He also noted that the School's contact with women's colleges had been chiefly through their landscape and botany departments instead of their art departments and thought this approach needed to be changed. Needless to say, it was. He summed up a rather long discussion as follows:

"I am as firmly convinced as I was twelve years ago that, for the best work in landscape, a practitioner needs a thorough grounding in the elements of architectural design and construction. The practitioners in both fields must learn to work hand in hand with mutual understanding and respect, if their clients are to be properly served....The present tendency within the School to be entirely landscape may be only temporary....There is not the slightest harm in having the majority of students take the landscape major. The School will suffer, however, if none take the architectural curriculum."

Bothered as he had been for some years by the term "Domestic Architecture" in the name of the School, he reported to the Trustees thus:

61

"While this title was an asset twelve years ago, we are likely to lose sight of the great strides that have been made by women in professional education and practice in the interim. They are, I believe, as naturally interested in domestic architecture today as they were when the School was founded, and turn from preference to such work in their practice. They do, however, resent any suggestion that they are not as capable of undertaking serious training as men. For this reason I have felt that the word "Domestic" has of late been a stumbling block, leading educators to think of us as teaching primarily small-house design, placing us, therefore, in their minds in the category of art schools and schools of interior decoration. If, in your opinion, this is true, the term "Domestic" should be removed from our title. Lest the Trustees think from these arguments that I have experienced a complete change of front, let me say that in the years I have watched this School develop, I have changed in only one fundamental principle. When Mr. Pond and I first started the School we had in mind a course which would train a student to design both houses and gardens by the simple method of teaching her only the design and construction of these units. It did not take us long to realize that in order to do distinguished work in this relatively small branch of the two professions a student needed a broad general training in the underlying principles of design and construction, and that this involved more extensive problems than the single house and its garden. For this reason, quite properly, our problems gradually included large units and groups of units. . . . The rapid development and expansion of landscape architecture throughout the country these past few years accompanied by the even greater and involved expansion in architecture leads me to feel that it is today presumptuous for the practitioner to attempt an equal practice in architecture and in landscape architecture, since this presumes an equal knowledge in the two professions. . . . I can no longer advise students to attempt a double practice. . . . The requirements of modern civilization are too complicated and exacting. It is, however, as true in my mind now as when the School started, that when the architectural features dominate in a problem the architect must have sufficient knowledge to control the general design of the setting and surroundings, and that when the landscape features of a problem dominate, the landscape architect equally must have the knowledge to control the architectural features of the design. In this fundamental principle, our School, I believe, strikes a new note in that it puts the principle into active practice."

Much of the comprehensive October 1928 report dealt with the financial situation of the School, a continuous need for more money. Starting, as it did, with no capital funds, no equipment, and very few resources to draw on, it is somewhat surprising that such a small school could remain in business. Always, however, it had had money enough to be satisfactorily solvent, never enough to do all of the things the Director and his faculty wanted to do. Although graduates and friends of the School had come to the rescue twice to clear small deficits, in 1928 the need was greater than ever. Apart from general running expenses, city taxes had been increased, and there was the matter of rent for the new building and the plan to buy the property at the end of five years. It would seem that only the most unshakable faith in the belief that women could be trained to be good architects and landscape architects and that The Cambridge School was the best place to train them could carry the Director and the many, many staunch friends of the School through this period.

Ending his report with suggested remedies for the situation, the Director restated two obvious alternatives for the future: 1) to remain an independent institution and work toward the goal of being able to grant advanced degrees, in part a matter of raising an endowment large enough to satisfy the authorities of Massachusetts; or 2) to become a graduate school of a woman's college capable of granting the desired advanced degrees. In the likelihood that the Trustees would opt for the second proposal, he listed fourteen specific provisos that in reality were a breakdown of the consensus of the earlier meeting with Mr. Neilson and possibly were included for his careful review.

Though not stated specifically, it was clearly implied that in any case The Cambridge School should remain in Cambridge as an autonomous entity. In addition to granting the degrees of Master of Architecture and Master of Landscape Architecture to qualified women from The Cambridge School, the women's college taking on this responsibility would be specifically asked to establish a number of tuition scholarships for students of the School. On the other side of the bargaining table the Director said that before any affiliation was undertaken The Cambridge School would 1) clear its deficit; 2) take title to the property now used for school purposes; and 3) raise a fund for equipment and operating purposes.

Apparently for the sake of weighing all possible solutions to the current dilemma, and watching with interest and perhaps amusement while they were tossed out, the Director offered several other alternative plans. The pros and cons of one he stated thus:

"Failing in either of the two plans already suggested we might become a graduate school of a college...by approaching it as a suppliant, asking it to assume our obligations, the building and grounds we now use, and the yearly deficit that seems certain to recur. In such a case we would be in no position to make demands....In all probability our appointments and salaries would be limited to such an extent that our teaching staff would seriously deteriorate. It might be impossible to retain certain of our instructors, and the usefulness and standing of the School might be seriously impaired....[This] plan seems to me not worthy of serious consideration if there is a determination to maintain and improve the teaching standards now existing...."

He added to the above suggestion one that would make the School a graduate school of some college *without* power to grant advanced degrees, perhaps seeking financial security and a future miracle in lieu of present academic solidity. Another suggestion was to try to keep the School as it was, clearing the deficit through greater publicity and more generous contributions. Still another and completely anachronistic proposal, which was significant in relation to the School at that particular time though not through its entire life, was that in order to save on salaries the School should give up, at least for a while, the architectural curriculum and train only landscape architects.

Possibly as a warning to the Trustees, the Director observed: "There is one advantage that we lose permanently if we become part of a women's college. At some time conditions may be such that we shall want to make the School co-educational. This would be impossible as a graduate school of a women's college." Little did he realize how soon women's colleges would be admitting men! Almost as an afterthought the very real person inside the greatly overworked Director appealed for help in carrying out his teaching responsibilities at Harvard and at The Cambridge School along with the heavy administrative responsibility of steering his favorite ship through some very precarious waters. He asked that four committees be appointed to handle financial matters, building and property, the library, and equipment.

---

[1]The Simmons affiliation was short lived, ending in 1934. At that time Lowthorpe proposed a complete merger with The Cambridge School, which was receptive to the idea but somewhat leery of the expense of maintaining the physical plant in Groton, always a formidable factor. The administrators tried to draw up a workable plan in which the assets of the two schools would be pooled together and their names combined. The difficulties they had encountered in the mid-1920's still existed, however, and after studying specific problems the Lowthorpe Board of Trustees withdrew its proposal with the comment that the plan "did not appear to be worked out as a merger of two going institutions, but rather as a complete takeover of Lowthorpe by The Cambridge School." In 1945, the school in Groton was closed, and Lowthorpe became the Lowthorpe Department of the Rhode Island School of Design in Providence.

[2]Not much ever came of the tentative plans at Columbia. A professional course in landscape architecture was established in the School of Architecture in 1934 but was dropped in 1945. During that time only two women received the Certificate of Proficiency in Landscape Architecture.

[3]As an example of continuing interest, the 1977 Commencement exhibition assembled and mounted by the Sophia Smith Collection (Women's History Archive) of Smith College was entitled "Green Space — Smith and Its Environment."

[4]A photograph of Miss Stoddard's 1914-15 class follows Chapter IV. The Botany Department stressed a need for studying ecology as well as systematic botany, thus predating the popular recognition of that subject by many years. If one can judge by another photograph, taken about the same time as the one of Miss Stoddard's class, it would seem that Miss Frances Grace Smith's students in ecology had been somewhat reluctant to follow her into the bog and had abandoned her to her hatted fate.

[5]Honoring its distinguished alumna, Smith's Ada Comstock Scholars Program enables women whose academic careers have been interrupted to complete their work for a B.A. degree. During the 1977-78 academic year, eighty-seven women were enrolled in the program.

[6]In the October 1928 report the courses offered at the School were grouped in five categories — Design, Construction, History, Freehand, and Miscellaneous Subjects. Summarized briefly (and losing much of the full flavor in condensation) they are described in Appendix A.

[7]Originally, the golden feline mascot of the drafting room, Henrietta Cantabrigia, had been named Henry, but after producing one lone kitten she was renamed. She was probably the most stretchable cat in history, and one of her greatest achievements was being able to retrieve a half-eaten sandwich from the bottom of an office wastebasket without moving her hind feet from the floor or upsetting the wastebasket.

Figure 4.1 — The Botanical Garden, core of the Smith College campus, with a glimpse of Paradise Pond. Dr. William Francis Ganong, first Director of the Botanical Garden, agreed with Smith's first President, Laurenus Clark Seelye, that the garden and campus should have scientific as well as aesthetic value.

Figure 4.2 — The first class in Landscape Architecture at Smith College, taught by Edna Stoddard (Ramseyer) during the academic year 1914-15. Smith's interest in landscape architecture as a profession for women predated affiliation with The Cambridge School by some twenty years.

Figure 4.3 — Frances Grace Smith of the Botany Department at Smith was a pioneer in teaching ecology. Though somewhat handicapped by her clothing, she appears to be undaunted in her search for treasures in a marsh. Her class seems to have lagged far behind.

Figure 4.4 — Kate Ries Koch, a graduate of Cornell University, taught landscape architecture at Smith from 1919 until her retirement in 1952. She was instrumental in having courses in landscape design transferred from the Botany Department to the Art Department and in establishing an inter-departmental major in landscape architecture.

Figure 4.5 — Karl Scott Putnam taught architecture at Smith from 1929 until his retirement as Associate Professor Emeritus in 1952. He was a great favorite among his students and encouraged many of them to continue in graduate work.

Figure 4.6 — Dorothy May Anderson, Resident Landscape
Architect and Assistant Professor at Smith from 1935 to 1943. She
is shown at her apartment near the campus, relaxing in/on her
"roof garden," which was mostly roof and very little garden.

5

The Waiting Years
1928-1932

From the exploratory Trustees' meetings of 1928 until affiliation with Smith College in 1932, everyone connected with The Cambridge School worked and waited. The period spanned both the stock market crash of 1929 and the depression that followed, usually thought of by those who lived through it as the Big Depression. It was not an easy time for raising large endowment funds or for instituting long-range plans. While the Trustees were weighing the advantages and disadvantages of affiliation with another institution, the alumnae were establishing a formal organization concerned primarily with ways to make money for the School. Members of the faculty were devising new and ever more challenging assignments for the students, who as usual, were working long hours and receiving honors. Only the Director knew what was going on on all fronts.

Problems of the Trustees

While the students were working and playing, the Trustees were struggling with long-range problems. Since the Director recommended that in any affiliation with another institution The Cambridge School should assume all financial responsibility in order to insure complete academic independence, the Trustees thought it imperative to assign highest priority to clearing a fairly small deficit and raising adequate operating funds. An unfortunate gap in the archival records of this period precludes our knowing exactly what measures were considered. The 1929 market crash probably dried up some potential sources of large private gifts, and at that time there were few foundations and no government endowments to help a small struggling school. Money coming in, in rather small amounts, cleared the deficit of 1928, and in 1929 the School squeaked through with a surplus of about $500, thanks to money raised by the newly organized Alumnae Association. For the next few years, however, operating expenses increased and so did the deficit. The optimism of the late 1920's was fast disappearing. In 1930, enrollment went up to seventy, mostly 3-year students but including some in special courses only. More teachers were added to the faculty and thus more money was spent for salaries. Taxes, rent, and extraordinarily high light bills were ever present, and each year more money went out for various incidental expenses that seemed unavoidable. It was obvious that charging more tuition was not the answer and would never make ends meet. Thus, as the School became better and better academically, its financial situation grew worse and worse.[1] President Neilson was not unaware of the financial difficulties The Cambridge School faced, but he thought that academic considerations were more important than the risks inherent in the situation, and he strongly favored an affiliation of the School with Smith College as soon as possible.

The Alumnae Association

Former students of The Cambridge School, particularly those who lived in the Boston area, had always kept in close touch with the School. Most of them knew each other and probably got together once in a while. Sometime before the end of 1928 they organized themselves into a formal association. Neither an exact date nor a Founder's List is available, but the movers behind the association probably included Edith Cochran, Laura Cox, Dorothea Harrison, Esther Kilton, Ethel Power, and Eleanor Raymond. In December 1928, Eleanor Raymond (over her signature as President of the Alumnae Association of The Cambridge School) wrote to all the alumnae about two important matters. First, she reported on the replies to an earlier letter she had written them about the Trustees' Meeting in October: thirty-eight of the forty-six alumnae who answered favored joining Smith College, and eight wanted to have the School remain independent. Second, the Executive Committee of the Trustees asked that the Alumnae Association raise $20,000 within the year. Part of this amount was to cover a current deficit and part was to start a fund to buy the new school building. She added that the Trustees were undertaking the raising of a much larger endowment fund. These funds were badly needed regardless of the School's future, which the Trustees wanted more time to discuss.

Apparently, no general fund-raising campaign was organized, and it is likely that the money received by the Alumnae Association was the result of a direct appeal to its members and their friends. By the spring of 1929 the group had about half the requested amount, and an anonymous donor promised to give $5,000 if the alumnae could raise

$15,000 by May 15. Through an urgent appeal, they did meet the $15,000 goal and received the anonymous "matching" gift. By fall of that year the Alumnae Association turned over more than the $20,000 asked of it. How well the Trustees had gotten on with their own attempt to raise an endowment fund is not recorded.

In December 1928 the Alumnae Association issued its first quarterly *Alumnae Bulletin.* By the end of the next year the organizers had compiled a comprehensive mailing list and announced an annual subscription rate of $2.00. The mimeographed *Bulletin* had been sent out free before, but obviously the Alumnae Association was not counting on subscriptions to channel money into the School's operating funds, since even by 1932 it had fewer than 300 members.[2] All The Cambridge School *Alumnae Bulletins* (which continued through July 1942) provided good reading matter. The first few covered mainly the activities of the students enrolled at the time, perhaps an attempt to let the alumnae working far afield know what was going on at the School and what changes had been made since they had left. The writers reported on the Summer School at Oxford and the honors won by seventeen Cambridge School students in the 1929 Landscape Exchange Problems. They noted the widespread geographic distribution in 1929 of the fifty students who came from thirty different institutions, as close as Radcliffe and as far away as the State of Washington and Bournemouth, England. It is not entirely clear who put together the earliest *Bulletins,* but by 1931 Louise Leland, Victorine duPont Homsey, Faith Bemis, and Edith Cochran were named as its editors. Naturally, a difference of opinion developed among recipients of the *Bulletin* as to what type of information should be emphasized. Everyone appreciated the personal news, reports on foreign and local study trips, and other items directly related to the School. They differed sharply on the value of substantive articles on design and construction. Some said that if they hadn't learned such things in school they could read professional magazines. The April 1932 issue, however, received general approval and praise for a long article on "Three Women in Landscape Architecture" by Clarence Fowler, who was on the Board of Trustees at that time. His three women were Beatrix Jones Farrand, Martha Brooks Hutcheson, and Marian C. Coffin, all of whom had entered the profession about 1900 and had built up and maintained very active and distinguished practices of their own.

In 1930 the Alumnae Association sent out a questionnaire to all past students. In a cover letter, Mr. Frost pleaded for complete information, saying that all questions were important, however irrelevant they might seem, and adding that he did not believe that marriage and professional careers were incompatible. "So," said he, "send us photos of your work and your children." Replies to this questionnaire as well as follow-up informal letters drifted in for two or three years.[3] They were virtually impossible to tabulate, as many women changed jobs during this time and new graduates became members of the Alumnae Association. It is obvious, however, that during the 1928-1932 period most graduates of The Cambridge School, both architects and landscape architects, were either practicing independently or in partnerships, or they were working in other professional offices, acquiring the apprenticeship experience so highly recommended. About half as many were involved in a wide range of other activities. Because jobs were not easy to find during the Depression years, some former students were continuing their studies abroad, and at least one was designing Christmas cards at home. Between those extremes, some Cambridge School women were working on the staffs of professional magazines or writing articles for them. One was writing a book [4]. Others were teaching, lecturing, and managing exhibitions of professional work.

Also in 1930 the Alumnae Association began a continuing appeal for contributions to help bolster the School funds. Establishing donor categories, as customary then as now, they asked the "Friends of the School" to give $10 a year and the "Guarantors" to give at least $100. In a note to the Friends, Mr. Frost remarked that if $10 seemed too much in a lump sum, perhaps a dollar a month would be less painful. The first year only $316 came in from the Friends, in contrast to the more than $20,000 raised a year or so before. No record is available on how much the Guarantors contributed, but obviously, the Depression was hitting hard all over.

The Director and His Faculty

The School had sponsored public lectures on "Modern Gardens" by Fletcher Steele and on "Modern Houses" by Jean Jacques Haffner in Boston, Washington, and Chicago. Those lectures probably account for some of the many letters received from garden clubs and other organizations asking for information about professional training. In answer to these frequent requests The Cambridge School in 1931 mounted a traveling exhibition including originals and prints of student work, photographs of work done by women practicing architecture and landscape architecture, photographs of English houses and gardens (no doubt requested by the Anglophile Director), pencil sketches by John Conant and Frank Rines, and water colors by Mary Gay. In all, the exhibition comprised more than 200 mounts, and much of the work behind the scenes fell on the faculty, as well as on all persuadable alumnae within reaching distance. Some 7500 copies of the official *Cambridge School Bulletin* and descriptive leaflets were sent out to announce The Cambridge School's Exhibition and Lecture Service. The School charged a fee of $40, "to defray costs of handling and of keeping the mounts in good condition," for the entire show, but it was willing to send out individual exhibits included in the show for as little as $5 each. The publicity folders also noted that if lectures were desired in connection with the exhibition, members of The Cambridge School faculty were available to give them. Those who spoke at various places that first year, for $50 plus expenses, were Henry A. Frost, Mary P. Cunningham, Harold Hill Blossom, Walter F. Bogner, and Stephen F. Hamblin. Of the thirty-four women who contributed photographs of their professional work, thirty were landscape architects. Perhaps the architects had more work coming in and were too busy to be sidetracked. Although most of the contributors were graduates of The Cambridge School and Lowthorpe, a few with backgrounds ranging from New York through the mid-west to California joined them[5]. The traveling Exhibition and Lecture Service went on for many years, and was considered to be a significant success.

The faculty had increased considerably since the spring of 1916, when it comprised two men in their office at 4 Brattle Street. The official *Cambridge School Bulletin* for the academic year 1930-31, selected by the author as recording a fairly typical year, lists seventeen more-or-less full-time members of the faculty and seven outside practitioners who gave special problems and thesis criticisms[6]. Almost half of them were also on the Harvard Faculty, and four of the six women teaching that year — Edith Cochran, Mary Cunningham, Anita Rathbun, and Eleanor Raymond — were graduates of The Cambridge School. The inclusion of William R. Sears among the special critics is misleading. He had been teaching full time since 1926 but was taking a year off to establish an office of his own in Boston. Also somewhat misleading, if the year is to be considered typical, is the inclusion of Margaret Burnham as the School's secretary. The "secretary" at 53 Church Street was actually an administrative officer, and most alumnae of that period remember Priscilla Loud Simonson, Louise Leland, or Dorothea MacMillan as holding the position. Miss Burnham was filling a short gap between the resignation of Mrs. Simonson and the appointment of Miss Leland.

Mr. Frost chose his faculty carefully, and having faith in those he chose, gave them a very free hand. They were a group of distinguished, hard-working men and women. In 1930-31, the design courses were taught by Professors Frost, Bogner, Newton, Fulkerson and their assistant, Anita Rathbun. Special problems were in the hands of Professors Haffner, Humphreys, and Pond and practitioners Blossom, Sears, and Raymond. They were truly dedicated teachers, advisors, and helpers, who gained much of their enthusiasm for the School's method of teaching from its Director. He, in turn, attributed the success of any school not just to its teachers but also to the quality of its students. In an introduction to an *Alumnae Bulletin* of 1930 he wrote:

> "...of no school can this be said more truly than of ours. The professions of architecture and landscape architecture have been, until very recent times, entirely in the hands of men. At present, women are not welcomed in many offices [even] as draughtsmen, and not a few practitioners are sincere in advising women not to attempt either profession. Therefore, a student entering the Cambridge School has to some degree the pioneering instinct [as well as] a modern viewpoint. She must realize that success in a field where men are receiving their training in long-established schools requires for her a training as good [as theirs]...and that with this training, because she is of necessity a pioneer, must go a high enthusiasm and an unusual tenacity of purpose. Our students do not drift into their professions along the lines of least resistance, nor do they drift through this school."

Indeed they didn't. The hasty lunches, if any, and the drafting-room lights burning well into the night indicated activity other than drifting[7].

Even as a relatively new member of the faculty, William R. Sears did much to strengthen the curriculum in Landscape Architecture. Although his speech at the ASLA Annual Meeting in January 1932 on the general status of the profession was not recorded (at least, no copy is available), he probably emphasized the thought, which he had expressed earlier to The Cambridge School Alumnae, that "the signs of the times indicate things are moving swiftly and the possibilities of landscape design are only just dawning." He led the School trip to Long Island in June, signing his report on the trip "Sole Survivor," and he also led a shorter trip to Nantucket in October. His death, at age forty, in November of that same year came as an incredible shock to all who worked with him and studied under him. In a tribute to him, Mr. Frost spoke of Dick Sears' constructive criticism and farsighted decisions. Many spoke of his unselfishness, cheerfulness, and his sense of humor, which was funny, delightful, and always free of any kind of malice. Mr. Frost summed up his relationship to the School thus:

> "Often reiterating that teaching was his avocation, not his life work, we who knew him used to smile because we had seen his enthusiasm when a student came up to his expectations, his patience when she did not, and his determination that the next effort would be more successful. He was a good teacher, which is high praise."

When James Sturgis Pray died on February 22, 1929, The Cambridge School had lost another very good friend. With the death of Professor Pray and the earlier death of Professor Warren, the two men of vision who had encouraged their young instructors to start a

76

professional school for women were gone. Professor Pray had begun teaching landscape architecture at Harvard in 1905 and, shortly before his death, had retired as Head of the Department of Landscape Architecture, a position he had held since 1913. His special interest was city planning, and in 1909 he had established the first formal course in City Planning taught in the United States. He was knowledgeable about all phases of landscape architecture and thought a well-trained, sensitive designer could make any outdoor space more livable and useful. Always active in the ASLA, Professor Pray held many of its offices, including the presidency from 1915 to 1918. He maintained a very keen interest in The Cambridge School until the day he died. He was only fifty-eight, and had he lived would no doubt have continued for many years to offer constructive advice on its progress. His death was a great personal loss to the Director.

Student Life

During the informal discussions of 1928, when President Neilson of Smith College met with The Cambridge School Trustees, it was agreed that all matters pertaining to the proposed affiliation be considered confidential until the proposal was either accepted or rejected. The knowledgeable ones on the inside — the Trustees, the administrative personnel, the members of the Council, some of the alumnae, and very likely most of the faculty — were certainly not talkative, and as far as one can tell after so long a time, there were no news leaks. The students were generally unaware of the School's uncertain future. They liked it the way it was and probably would have looked on any proposed change as a potential menace, an infringement upon their hectic, disorderly, and thoroughly satisfying routine. Looking back, the situation seems somewhat surprising, as the students, faculty, and administrative officers were a closely knit group and there must have been many chances for a slip of the tongue. Mrs. Frost was generous and gracious in bringing faculty and students together for social gatherings, although she was busy bringing up two small sons and had many outside interests of her own. A few of the students were close friends of some of the "insiders," and some had direct contact with the Front Office through part-time typing jobs or responsibilities in connection with running a small drafting-room supply shop[8].

Occasionally the students had time to enjoy the spacious backyard that came with the new quarters on Church Street, and during the summer sessions at Rockport they relaxed on the beaches of Cape Ann. Sometime about 1930 a phonograph appeared in the downstairs drafting room. This was indeed an innovation, and the advanced students upstairs made a few unkind remarks about the noise downstairs being an unsuitable atmosphere for real work. Soon, however, a phonograph appeared in the upstairs drafting room, too.

Mr. Frost, whose office in the older part of the building was midway between the two, complained that hearing jazz from below and Beethoven from above left something to be desired in his own working conditions[9].

No description of life at The Cambridge School would be complete without a salute to Mr. Geary, the janitor and friend to all students. He stoked the furnace, cut the grass, coped with unbelievable trash (some of which the owner considered to be treasure) in the drafting rooms, took care of the pets, mended all sorts of school equipment and personal gadgets, and one year planted a magnificent border of magenta phlox and orange marigolds in the backyard. The Director remarked that it was the only color scheme the students had not yet tried on their water-color renderings.

The hard work in the drafting rooms and classrooms went on very much as it had before and would continue to go on. Design problems, which were assigned to a group and were always somewhat competitive, were never graded by the instructor in charge but were objectively judged by a jury including other faculty members, usually the Director, and often professional men and women not connected with the School. When the students assembled to listen to the resulting critiques, both faculty and students benefited from the analysis of the judgments. They were told why some solutions received high marks and praise whereas others were tossed out completely — or so nearly completely that it made little difference to the student who had worked on the problem maybe a week, maybe six or eight weeks, and being very close to questions involved found it hard to agree with the rating of the jury. Sometimes the same problems were assigned to the men at Harvard and the women at The Cambridge School, and each group had a chance to see how the other was progressing.

Many disappointments, and occasionally a few tears, marked the aftermath of each jury session, but they seemed to have no adverse effect on the relationship between student and teacher. This relationship was based on mutual respect and an understanding that the student really wanted to learn and that the teacher wanted very much to help her. The general atmosphere of interest in everybody's work and the feeling that the best answer must be found to everybody's specific difficulties had not changed much since the earliest days of the office-school. Edward A. Varney and Edith Cochran were hard taskmasters in construction, as Charles Killam and other instructors had been before them. Stephen Hamblin and Mary Cunningham were just as strict about all phases of knowing and using plants skillfully. Both had been thoroughly trained and were prolific writers. It seemed to many an astonished student that the scientific names of plants they bandied about so freely (and were so hard for others to learn) must be coming to them from voices out of the blue. While conducting field trips, teachers of construction and plant materials seemed strangely insensitive to the hazards of heat stroke or frozen feet, to say nothing of aching muscles. Faculty and students alike were pleased that Mary Gay's water colors were receiving wide acclaim and that Frank Rines was writing and illustrating a book[10]. Although all freehand courses were considered to be basic necessities, many students found they were refreshing recreation — unless, that is, if in the life drawing classes held in the evening one was not too tired to figure out which leg went where. To the students, the faculty often seemed intrepid and very demanding, but the alleviating factor that held them all together was the slow but sure glue of patience. The School seemed to have a knack for collecting persons with endless patience.

Usually, the Director himself was a very patient man. There were times, however, when Henry A. Frost could, and did, rapidly reduce a student to a soggy pulp with a few biting comments about her work. Sometimes his unexpected harshness was related to the truly poor quality of the work under scrutiny, something he judged to be unworthy of the student's ability and the principles that she, presumably, had learned. As one got to know him and his moods better, however, most students realized that often they just happened to be in the way when the frustrations of an overworked and worried administrator had reached a temporary limit. Invariably, the student who happened to be there when the dam burst was singled out later for a little extra encouragement and special praise when it was justified. Also without exception, if one can judge by conversations, correspondence, and replies to questionnaires, no student left The Cambridge School without a sense of gratitude and a lifelong devotion to its Director.

The Rockport Summer School

Probably the most exciting event of this period was the purchase of a very attractive old house at 7 South Street, Rockport, late in 1931. The property was bought by "an anonymous donor," who was later discovered to be Anita Rathbun (Mrs. Harlan W. Bucknell), then a familiar person in the drafting room. She appropriated money for alterations and improvements, including the conversion of a large garage into a drafting room for twenty students. It was agreed that Mr. Frost would rent the house for his family's summer home with the understanding that the place would be used as a Summer School for six weeks each year. Mr. and Mrs. Frost spent every weekend during the winter and early spring of 1932 working on the house and grounds, and with the able help of Ralph Berger, the School's librarian, they had it ready for the Grand Opening on May 21, 1932. In Cambridge, students and faculty alike were ecstatic at the prospect of getting away from the sultry heat of Harvard Square, and Nature cooperated with gusto: That May 21st was the coldest in Cape Ann's history. With fires in all the fireplaces, it was a literal housewarming as the Frosts welcomed sixty-five persons, including honored guests, faculty, alumnae, and the thirty-three students enrolled for the summer session. At dinner, Dorothy May Anderson, the toastmistress, introduced Mr. C. Howard Walker, the main speaker, and several other friends of The Cambridge School. The Rockport Summer School was officially established and ready for business.

The town of Rockport was ideal for the freehand classes in both pencil sketching and water color offered to advanced students; and assignments in the new drafting room introduced students entering The Cambridge School for the first time to the basics of design and construction. The buildings, the small formal garden restored and cared for by Edith Cochran, and the great sweep of open lawn and meadow sloping down to the beach were a joy to generations of students. And as Mr. Frost remarked, with the frugal New England side of his temperament uppermost for the moment, it had all been accomplished through the generosity of an anonymous alumna and thus had not increased the financial obligations of The Cambridge School in "these difficult times"[11].

---

[1] In today's world a parallel can be seen among the many small private schools, museums, theaters, and art groups of all sorts. As excellence in each particular field is achieved and recognized and the public is thereby better served, expenses increase and the small institutions must spend far too much time on frantic fund drives and other efforts to keep afloat financially.

[2] Although not a valid comparison, one can note that at that time the Smith College Alumnae Association numbered about 13,000.

[3] The questions posed in 1930 were not unlike those posed by the ASLA Committee for Women in Landscape Architecture in October 1976. These were circulated with a request that replies be sent in before Thanksgiving of that year, but they dribbled in through January 1979. Whether this indicates that Cambridge School women are naturally dilatory or doggedly persevering is hard to say.

[4] Eleanor Raymond's *EARLY DOMESTIC ARCHITECTURE OF PENNSYLVA-NIA*, was first published in 1931 and republished in 1973.

[5] For those who are interested in knowing about some, but not all, of the women who were practicing architecture and landscape architecture at that time, the contributors in 1931 were Mary Almy, Mabel Keyes Babcock, Anne Baker, Katherine Bashford, Margaret Eaglesfield Bell, Marjorie Sewell Cautley, Marian Coffin, Elizabeth Coit, Mary P. Cunningham, Florence Holmes Gerke, Annette Hoyt Flanders, Helen Gail, Rose Greely, Victorine duPont Homsey, Lois Lilley Howe, Helen Swift Jones, Rosalind Spring La Fontaine, Elizabeth Lord, Margaret Manning, Carina Eaglesfield Mortimer, Elizabeth G. Pattee, Louise Payson, Isabella Pendleton, Constance Peters, Henrietta Marquis Pope, Eleanor Raymond, Catherine Jones Richards, Edith Schryver, Ellen Shipman, Clara I. Thomas, Helen Van Pelt, Helene B. Warner, and Beatrice Williams.

[6] The names of all the Faculty members as well as members of The Cambridge School Council and the Board of Trustees in 1930-31 are included in Appendix B.

[7] A notice on the bulletin board in the fall of 1930 read: "As is well known, the School is meticulous in observing legal holidays. On Armistice Day there will be no lectures. The drafting rooms will be open from 8 a.m. until midnight."

[8] The students did know that the School needed money (who didn't?), and occasionally bets were placed on the many visitors who came through the drafting rooms — bets on

whether they were "ways" or "means". If the visitors took the students as they were, with no questioning glances at trashy tables and grubby faces, they were chalked up as "ways," friends who came to see how the work was getting on. If, however, they were preceded by a gentle warning from the Front Office to tidy up a bit, the students hung up hazardous T-squares, kicked the wastebaskets out of the main aisle, perhaps rubbed a smock tail over a dirty face (nothing could be done about hands and fingernails), and made a fairly safe bet that the approaching visitor was a "means".

[9] The rather special spontaneous hilarity created among students everywhere was not lacking at The Cambridge School. One alumna remembers a cram session before a history exam. One of the students apparently had a mental block that prevented her from correctly identifying English country houses. Her mentors suggested that she could certainly remember Hatfield House because the finials along the wall looked like hats. When her turn came on the oral part of the exam, she did indeed draw a slide of Hatfield House and promptly said, with great confidence, "Derbyshire". An answer on another exam, in construction, probably amused the instructors more than the student, who happened to be a poor speller, when she wrote: "Every swimming pool should have a waist control, conveniently yet inconspicuously located." The gaffe that became something of a slogan, however, was the advice of an instructor in Professional Practice who, in suggesting the best way to find a job, said: "Go out and sell yourself to an architect."

[10] *DRAWING IN LEAD PENCIL,* Frank M. Rines, Bridgman Publishers, Pelham, N.Y., 1929.

[11] The permanent residents and long-time summer people of Rockport were used to artists of all types and took the sketching classes in stride. They were curious, however, about those girls lugging around surveying equipment in the most unlikely places. One day the curiosity of a few watchers was rewarded by the scene in a nearby pasture. The girls were apparently surveying two cows, two horses, and one long-legged colt. The colt in a friendly mood frisked across the pasture and knocked over the tripod and plane table, scattering instruments in all directions, while the girls tried vainly to persuade his mother to come and get him. Better by far, however, than the previous summer surveys of Belmont Hill in all its heat and traffic!

That first summer, many visitors arrived to see what the school was all about. This tended to complicate life for Mrs. Frost, as she had taken on the responsibility of providing some of the meals for the students. She found they had appalling appetites. Being a gracious, friendly person, she was always happy to have the students come, but by the end of the term she was equally happy to see them go.

No. 7 South Street is now a pleasant inn; the former drafting room has been converted to sleeping quarters.

Figure 5.1 — Isabelle De Courcy Porter, alumna of Smith College and The Cambridge School, maintained a successful practice in Boston for many years. She was an enthusiastic supporter of The Cambridge School Alumnae Association and in other ways helped the school progress. Her boat afforded many happy hours of relaxation, as she was an excellent sailor as well as a good landscape architect.

Figure 5.2 — Henry A. Frost in his office at 53 Church Street.

Figure 5.3 — "Si" (Albert E.) Simonson, architect and favorite teacher of many students at The Cambridge School, contemplating a problem that was no doubt solved eventually.

Figure 5.4 — Mary Gay, humorous and indomitable in the face of all obstacles, whose inspiring classes in water color were often hilarious.

Figure 5.5 — Carol Fulkerson, landscape architect, who through his teaching at The Cambridge School, Lowthorpe, and the Rhode Island School of Design encouraged many of the professional women in landscape architecture today.

Figure 5.6 — Mary P. Cunningham at her graduation from Vassar in 1910. A student, teacher, and knowledgeable advisor she was an active and important part of The Cambridge School from 1917 until her death in 1934.

Figure 5.7 — Henry A. Frost advising one of his students. All students appreciated his critical mind, unswerving professionalism, and personal sympathy.

Figure 5.8 — Some take the high road, as Elizabeth Campbell did while drafting a hard-to-reach detail.

Figure 5.9 — Some take the low road, as Josie Conant believed was necessary for precision.

Figure 5.10 — Sam Hershey's class sketching in the backyard of The Cambridge School at 53 Church Street. It was always called the yard, never the garden.

Figure 5.11 — The yard provided for relaxation. Presumably, Polly Spencer (Groves), Fran Whitmore (Burgess), Cary Millholland (Parker), Grace Hight (Kirkwood), and reclining Hope Slade (Jansen) have finished their assigned problems as well as their lunch.

Figure 5.12 — Janet Darling (Webel) near the door of the drafting-room wing while a student at 53 Church Street. Later she became a distinguished landscape architect in New York and, in 1959, was elected a Fellow of the ASLA.

Figure 5.13 — Maud Sargent sketching somewhere near Cambridge.

Figure 5.14 — Mr. Geary, called janitor for want of a better title, was indispensable to the school in all its official homes. He was furnaceman, chauffeur, yardman, painter, gadget repairman, wizard remover of trash, chainsmoker of cigars, and in all a rugged individual. Here he is seen with one of the many pets he cared for while their owners were busy in the drafting room.

Figure 5.15 — No. 7 South Street, Rockport, the Frost's summer home after 1931 and headquarters of the Rockport Summer School.

Figure 5.16 — Hope Slade (Jansen), Fran Whitmore (Burgess), and Georgia Hencken (Perkins) enjoying lunch at Rockport.

Figure 5.17 — Anna Lochman Frost, gracious hostess who enthusiastically welcomed the summer students when they came to Rockport but who also appreciated the peace and quiet when they left. Her tactful advice behind the scenes and the social occasions she arranged helped make The Cambridge School run smoothly.

Figure 5.18 — Part of the garden between the house and the drafting room at the Rockport Summer School.

Figure 5.19 — No finer place could be found for Dorothy May Anderson to perch while sketching than the fence post at 7 South Street, Rockport.

Figure 5.20 — G. Holmes Perkins, architect, and his class on the beach at Rockport. It is hard to say whether the students are studying architectural design, pencil sketching, or rest and relaxation.

6

The Solution: Affiliation 1932-38

The Cambridge School Board of Trustees met on May 11, 1932, to discuss the final terms of the proposal for affiliation with Smith College, a draft of which had been approved by The Cambridge School Council in April. Present at this decisive meeting of the Trustees were Albert Farwell Bemis, Walter H. Kilham, John Nolen, Amelia Peabody, Bremer Pond, Paul J. Sachs, Romney Spring (Treasurer), Fletcher Steele, Henry A. Frost (President), and Louise Leland (Secretary). Proxies had been received from Laurence Curtis II, and Clarence Fowler. Professor George H. Edgell had recently resigned from the Board because of increased responsibilities at Harvard, and Mrs. William Morton Wheeler had resigned because of illness. The School had lost one of its most interested and sympathetic Trustees when Professor Byron S. Hurlbut died in 1930.

The Proposal

This nine-point proposal brought before the meeting incorporated most of the things discussed and informally agreed upon at the two exploratory meetings in 1928[1]. The School was to remain in Cambridge and was to be known as The Cambridge School of Architecture and Landscape Architecture, An Affiliated Graduate School of Smith College. The granting of Master's degrees by Smith College for college graduates who had finished the full curriculum at The Cambridge School was spelled out in detail, as was the awarding of Certificates by The Cambridge School for those who had completed the same requirements but did not hold Bachelor's degrees. The business of actually running the School and paying the bills fell solely upon The Cambridge School. Smith College assumed no financial responsibilities.

Coordination of policies was to be in the hands of The Cambridge School Council working with "not less than one nor more than two" members of the Board of Trustees of Smith College. The President of Smith was to be a member of The Cambridge School Board of Trustees ex officio, without limit of time. The final point was that "the academic direction of the School be in the hands of the School Faculty as heretofore, subject to such control from the College as the two institutions shall agree is for their mutual benefit."

The proposal for affiliation with Smith College was adopted unanimously but not without some interesting comments. One such was a suggestion that the School be moved either permanently or for the duration of the Depression to Rockport, Massachusetts. Taken out of context of past discussions, this seems an amazing idea, but in context it was considered to be a way of reducing expenses, perhaps mistakenly so. The suggestion of moving was discarded on several long-range counts: that the academic and cultural facilities so readily available in Cambridge but not in Rockport were a distinct advantage to the School (Mr. Pond reminded the Board again that many of Lowthorpe's problems stemmed from its location in a small town); that enrollment probably would go down; that there was no guarantee that over the years the financial gain would offset the disadvantages; and that the proposed affiliation with Smith might well be jeopardized by moving to a location even more remote from Northampton than Cambridge.

Dropping the word "Domestic" from the name of the School, in the proposal, seemed to be a stumbling block for some, as it had been for years. One Trustee who wanted to retain the term wondered whether a Master's degree could not be given in Domestic Architecture, but others doubted that there was any such precedent and also doubted whether the American Institute of Architects (AIA) would recognize such a limited part of the profession. In the end the decision was left to the discretion of the Smith College Board of Trustees. They evidently approved the deletion, and so after years of prodding by the Director, "Domestic" disappeared from the School's name, never to return.

A few Trustees still dwelt unrealistically on the abortive attempt to affiliate with Radcliffe — the friend, neighbor, and college of their choice. They were somewhat reassured by the fact that Miss Comstock was on the School Council and also on Smith's Board of Trustees. Apparently one or two of the group hesitated about making a major commitment at that particular time and wondered whether the curricula at The Cambridge School really measured up to those that led to Master's degrees in other well-known institutions. The Director assured them that the School did measure up in all landscape work and that the only weakness in the architectural curriculum was in advanced construction, a course that was being strengthened at that time. His appraisal was strongly endorsed by Bremer Pond, who said the School held its own very well indeed when compared to Harvard and M.I.T. and who also cited examples of comparable work at widely known institutions in other parts of the United States. Paul Sachs said that President Neilson's interest in the School was a tribute to its growth and value, and that he knew from his own experience on the Smith Board of Trustees, that the Board was in sympathy with Mr. Neilson's views. He suggested that the thanks of The Cambridge School Board be expressed to Mr. Neilson for his confidence in the School and for the privilege he offered it through an affiliation.

Presumably heart-felt thanks to President Neilson from many people went along with the proposal for affiliation, and on June 18, 1932 the Smith College Board of Trustees voted to accept it. In September, the Smith Board named Harriet Bliss Ford as its first member to serve on The Cambridge School Board, along with Mr. Neilson. It was a fortunate choice. Mrs. Ford had an innate administrative skill, not always appreciated by those involved, in untangling tricky situations. As the wife of George B. Ford, a noted planner, she had spent much of her life in the world of architecture, landscape architecture, and planning. She recognized the overall problems in these fields, and she knew the jargon as well as the language of design.

Life at The Graduate School in Cambridge

As an Affiliate of Smith College, The Cambridge School went along much the same as it had before affiliation. The drafting rooms were filled with new students. Most of them, and most of the faculty as well, were working on a very large model of Middlesex Village, a teaching device that affected all courses in both disciplines.[2] The project was based on an actual nearby site that had been chosen by Professors Simonson and Fulkerson. In a series of competitive problems, the students designed the general layout and also made detailed plans for more than a hundred houses. The technical execution of the model itself was greatly dependent upon Ralph Berger, an experienced cabinet maker who had come to The Cambridge School as its librarian. His shock of white hair and his pince-nez glasses on a black ribbon lent distinction to the library, but his great love affair was with the Middlesex Village model and its complicated requirements for perfection. The library suffered at first but was soon put under the very competent care of Mrs. Frost. As each term ended, the precocious students left a little before the official closing time, with their work neatly completed, but some students whose academic standing was a bit precarious usually left in a shambles of last-minute packing and incomplete work, which was bound to bring bad news when they returned.

Mr. Frost thought the students were feeling the Depression along with everyone else in that he saw more of them on stools at the quick lunch counters than around the tables at the Cock Horse, though this may well have been merely a matter of saving time when work pushed too hard. He regretted that even the Depression had little effect on the large quantities of tracing paper tossed in waste baskets every day and the half-used pencils and erasers left lying around. Like the architect and city planner Daniel H. Burnham, he was cheered by "big plans that stir men's souls," but he was truly distressed by waste in any form. In their general outlook on life, the New Englander Henry A. Frost and the Scot William A. Neilson were more than affiliates — they were cut from the same cloth.

A number of English students studied at The Cambridge School, either on their own or through an exchange scholarship with the Architectural Association School in London. Among them was Juliet Inego-Triggs, whose father had been a well-known architect and writer whose greatest interest really was designing gardens. His home was always open to members of the summer study groups as well as other Cambridge School women studying or traveling in England. Though at least one of the English women remained to practice in the United States, most of them returned to England and practiced there, sometimes after several years of life in the "Colonies". Some, but not as many, American women from The Cambridge School studied at the Architectural Association School in London.

One unusually cold winter evening, a few students (architects, obviously, surely not landscape architects) shoveled snow and flooded part of the backyard at 53 Church Street for a skating rink fifty feet square. When morning came the shoveled space was clear with only a thin film of ice, and a large block of ice a foot or so thick was lodged securely in a snowbank several yards away from the clearing. The landscape construction students scarcely needed to point out (but they did) that the skaters had chosen the only slightly sloping part of the yard for their rink. That winter a trip through either drafting room was unusually hazardous because of the many pairs of skates hung over table lights along with other paraphernalia, and the Director supposed he could be grateful that the students had not yet taken up indoor golf. Thus the banter between the Front Office and the drafting rooms continued, and despite moments of hilarity, the students continued to work hard, and their efforts continued to be recognized with praise and honors.

Smith College Commencement, 1934

The period of uncertainty about degrees had formally ended, and the most outstanding event of the first years of affiliation was the Smith College Commencement of June 1934. The College awarded the degrees of Master of Architecture to twenty women and Master of Landscape Architecture to twenty-nine, all of whom had been certified by The Cambridge School. Some of these women, including Katherine Brooks Norcross, Frances Jackson, Elizabeth D. Jones, and Gertrude Sawyer had been among the very first students at the Frost and Pond office and its various annexes between 1915 and 1920. In 1935, one Master of Architecture and seven Master of Landscape Architecture degrees were granted to Cambridge School candidates, five of whom had been practicing for several years[3]. From then on, with a few exceptions, the candidates who were presented for Smith College degrees each year had finished their Cambridge School theses within the year. Many of the women who were eligible for Master's degrees in 1934 had been practicing successfully for many years without a degree and chose not to join the group. Others who had received Certificates from The Cambridge School on the basis of requirements fulfilled could not be granted advanced degrees because they did not hold Bachelor's degrees[4].

The 1934 Commencement was indeed a celebration, not only for the women whose work was recognized at long last but also for Mr. Frost and Mr. Neilson, who had done much to make the day possible. The evening before the ceremonies, Mr. and Mrs. Frost were honored at a dinner at The Manse, where Dorothea Harrison was toastmistress. Later, the assembled group of Cambridge School people and many Smith visitors went to see the exhibition of student renderings and the model of Middlesex Village on display at the Hillyer Art Gallery. The next morning, as The Cambridge School women formed a group in the Commencement procession, an onlooker was overheard to say, with some surprise, "Why, they're really a nice looking lot!"

The Faculty

The roster of faculty members changed from time to time during the period of affiliation but maintained the established pattern of mostly Harvard professors with a few instructors from professional offices. Robert Beal finished teaching the design courses started by Dick Sears in the fall of 1932, and the next spring Morley J. Williams joined the faculty on a more permanent basis. Another landscape architect, Frederick S. Kingsbury, came in the fall of 1933. Albert E. Simonson, always known as "Si," and Holmes Perkins were teaching architectural design. In 1938, Marc Peter came to teach the course in Interior Architecture that had been established in 1935. Edith Cochran taught landscape construction, plant materials, and planting design. To give a more rounded approach with less duplication, Carol Fulkerson and Holmes Perkins combined and taught the five history courses as one general course. Professor Charles Killam rejoined the faculty, after several years absence, to teach landscape construction, leaving Edward A. Varney more time for architectural construction. Mary Gay was still vigorously leading her water color classes, and Samuel Hershey, who had replaced Frank Rines, was teaching pencil sketching. During the 1932-38 period, critics who were called in and who devastated many "brilliant solutions" to theoretical and practical problems alike included Radford Abbott, Walter Bogner, Jean Jacques Hafner, Justin Hartzog, and Samuel Homsey.

In 1934, Mary P. Cunningham was killed in a bizarre street accident in Boston. Her classes were taken over temporarily by Robert S. Sturtevant and William B. Marquis and were later taught by Edith Cochran. Mary P. Cunningham had been among the first group of students who formed The Cambridge School even before it had a name other than "The Little School," and she had taught plant materials and planting design since 1919. She seemed an intrinsic part of The Cambridge School. Miss Cunningham had also taught at Smith College and at Lowthorpe and therefore was a knowledgeable link among the three institutions. Her death was a staggering blow to everyone. Aside from contacts through her teaching, the faculty and students knew her well through friendly visits to her office and her home in Boston. They also knew her through many articles in professional magazines. Although a stickler for sound technical knowledge, she insisted that the mere learning of plant names was not enough and that the real purpose of studying plants was to develop an appreciative knowledge of their qualities in terms of design. Mary P. Cunningham was a fascinating teacher, and though warm appreciation for her courses was sometimes tempered by a cold lack of enthusiasm for tramping about the Arnold Arboretum in all kinds of weather, she was a great favorite at the School. Like students before and since when speaking of their favorites, hers seldom spoke of a course in plant materials but only of "taking Miss Cunningham."

The summer trips for study abroad had been very popular and interest in them continued, but the 1930's were uncertain times in Europe. An unfortunate gap in Cambridge School records of the mid-1930's precludes detailed reporting, but some general information is available. Two trips planned for 1933 — the fourth one to England and the first covering Central Europe and Scandinavia — were cancelled because of political conditions abroad. In 1934, some dozen or so students studied while traveling throughout Italy, and in 1936 the Central Europe and Scandinavia trip was rescheduled for a larger group, who went only to Scandinavia and, somewhat surprisingly, to Germany. Several of the alumnae who traveled on their own during the uncertain '30's found the carefully prepared itineraries for Cambridge School study trips very helpful, and through letters to the *Alumnae*

Bulletin they described their experiences for the less fortunate souls who were left at home. Though no one knew how he could find the time, Mr. Frost led most of the study trips abroad himself, with some help from other faculty members who went along.

Alumnae Activities

The hard task of raising money for scholarships and other expenses continued to fall on the alumnae of The Cambridge School. In its barely twenty years the small school had acquired an immensely enthusiastic group of graduates, but they were still relatively few and were busy women scattered all over the country. Ironically, it was a critical period partly because the School's twin goals of many years had been achieved: The School was finally housed in more than adequate quarters at Cambridge and Rockport, and the student's work was now recognized by the awarding of academic degrees. Complacency could have set in easily. But more students working toward degrees needed scholarships, and the buildings had to be maintained and eventually paid for. The Alumnae Association continued to work on the series of School-sponsored public lectures begun a few years before, and as a new venture, the group opened a House and Garden Center in Boston.

Frank Lloyd Wright, under the sponsorship of The Cambridge School, lectured at Jordan Hall in November 1932. A dramatically impressive though controversial figure, he was generally popular, and it was his first appearance in Boston. The contract for the lecture had been signed only two weeks earlier, and the alumnae in charge of publicity, Eleanor Raymond and Ethel Power, were hard pressed. They received unexpected help, however, from the local press, which on the day of the lecture published rumors about a plot to kidnap the great architect. Jordan Hall was filled almost to capacity, and although a few malcontent students heckled the speaker from the balcony, the event was a great success. It netted about $300 for the School. The next year Rockwell Kent and Frau Von Tippleskirk, a German architect, also drew good crowds in Boston. In New York, the alumnae sponsored a separate series of lectures by Henry A. Frost, Fletcher Steele, Carol Fulkerson, and two Cambridge School alumnae — Helen Swift Jones and Elizabeth Meade. Helen Swift Jones was doing well in her practice in New York and Betty Meade was then teaching courses in landscape architecture at Vassar. The New York alumnae also sponsored a series of three lectures by Ellen Shipman, and the Boston group offered a similar "short-course" series by Elsa Rehmann and Stephen F. Hamblin.

The House and Garden Center at 127 Newbury Street not only sold all sorts of garden and household gadgets (donations came in from all over the country), but as a drawing card the Center also maintained a small reference library and exhibition space and gave clinical advice to homeowners who were uncertain about how to improve their surroundings. The clients paid $1.00 for a single session of advice at the Center and $5.00 for six short informal lectures by volunteer alumnae in the Boston group[5]. The women also organized round-table discussions about common problems. The whole activity was good publicity for the School, and the volunteers hoped that it might lead to more jobs for themselves. Financially, the Center was a success. On the opening day in December 1934, it took in $800, a fine figure for those days. During its four-year existence it consistently turned over substantial sums to the Scholarship Fund. Minding the store, however, is always a trying and tiring task, and by mid-1935 the volunteers were exhausted from the unrelenting schedule they had devised for themselves. An outside manager, Alice Alden, was put in charge and the Center continued through the spring of 1938, when Miss Alden left to be married. At that time an obituary notice for the House and Garden Center was run in the *Alumnae Bulletin*.

In the best tradition of alumnae fund workers, The Cambridge School alumnae sponsored local exhibitions and various social affairs in addition to the lecture series and the Center, and they sold magazine subscriptions. They stopped just short of selling apples on street corners, but they found no enormous pots of gold at the end of any of their rainbows. It wasn't that the projects were unworthy or unsound but merely that too much work fell on too few people. Nor did the direct appeal for money fall on deaf ears, but the amounts that came in from all sources were always smaller than anticipated.

By 1933 the *Alumnae Bulletin* was in the extraordinarily capable hands of Louise Leland, an alumna of both Smith College and The Cambridge School, who at that time was the Director's administrative assistant. She sent out another appeal for information about alumnae activities. The responses presented much the same picture as the replies to the 1930 questionnaire, except that for the first time, some of the alumnae were working on public projects. Of the eighty-two women who reported on their work in the mid-30's, thirty-nine had opened offices of their own or were in partnership with others; twenty were working in larger well-established professional offices; thirteen were working on public projects, chiefly parks in New York and New Haven, and ten were teaching landscape architecture at both undergraduate and graduate levels. Most of these women in the mainstream of the profession were working on the eastern seaboard, in every state from Maine to Florida, (except rather surprisingly, Pennsylvania and South Carolina), and in the District of Columbia. A fair number, however, were working in California, Oregon, South Dakota, New Mexico, Kentucky, Tennessee, Illinois, Michigan, and Ohio, and in England.

Others who wrote to the *Alumnae Bulletin* in 1933 were marking time along the fringes of the profession. Ten were lecturing or giving short interviews on radio; nine were writing books or articles, working in bookshops, or exhibiting work they had done; five were working in nurseries; and one was doing historical research on Colonial estates of the South. Two were pursuing higher goals through advanced studies at Cranbrook and Taliesen. Two, Edith Cochran and Dorothea Harrison, were taking an active part in the Boston Chapter of ASLA and were urging others to join and do likewise. Those who had married and had given up their professional work, at least temporarily, were not so likely to write to the *Bulletin*. Mary Linder was an exception, as she wrote exciting letters from the Belgian Congo, where she and her husband, Patrick Tracy Putnam, were living while doing anthropological research on the Pygmies of the Ituri Forest.

Until the mid-1930's virtually all landscape architects, at least all women in the field, were specializing in private estates. When government projects began to alleviate widespread unemployment, new and different jobs became available. Some of The Cambridge School graduates were pioneers in the larger scale projects of that period. Mary Duguid went to work for the Tennessee Valley Authority (TVA) and was joined later by Wenonah Sibley. Eliza Birnie worked for the National Capital Parks and Planning Commission in Washington, D.C., and later for the National Forest Service, not then known for hiring women. In New York, as part of a plan to set 70,000 unemployed people to work, Commissioner Moses set up a group of forty landscape architects in the loft of the Madison Square Garden Building to rehabilitate the city's park system. Many of these landscape architects were women, and six of them — Alma Alison, Eleanor Jones, Helen Swift Jones, Rosalind Spring LaFontaine, Maud Sargent, and Cynthia Wiley — were from The Cambridge School. The pay scale set up for the landscape architects on this project were somewhat lower than that for bricklayers, but enthusiasm for their job seemed to more than compensate for the lack of financial gain.

The alumnae, faculty, and students of The Cambridge School gathered together at least once a year for Alumnae Day, which began with sketch problems, quizzes, and exhibitions and was climaxed by the annual dinner. Committees in charge had a knack for finding guests who were exceptionally good speakers, and the entire day seemed rather like a meeting of a mutual admiration society. Pleasant as they were, however, these annual events within a closed circle did very little to publicize the School.

Publicity (the term Public Relations had not yet come into common usage) was handled in several ways. Cambridge School pamphlets were handed out at the Smith College booth at the Century of Progress

Exposition in Chicago in 1933. A rather handsome booklet on the history of the School, illustrated by students' sketches, renderings, and photographs of models as well as photographs of work executed by several alumnae, was assembled by the alumnae under the critical eye of Harriet Bliss Ford and published in 1936. Some 2,500 copies, costing an extravagant total of $1,000, were distributed where they presumably had a favorable impact on prospective students. The booklet did not, however, prove to be an effective magnet for wealthy patrons. The Middlesex Village model and others went on the road from time to time in connection with lectures and exhibitions. These models engendered considerable interest, but the costly and time-consuming job of packing and transporting them was appalling. Henry A. Frost and Louise Leland were popular speakers on the lecture circuit, which covered an amazingly large area[6]. Informal talks and round-table discussions on house and garden problems were well attended wherever one or more alumnae were at hand to organize them. All in all The Cambridge School was becoming better known throughout the country. Increasing tuition enough to cover expenses during those lean years was virtually impossible, and it seemed that the more students there were the more help the School needed to keep up its standards. Since no one had come forth with a large, or even a barely adequate, endowment, hopes for erasing the deficit grew very faint.

Changes at Smith College

Smith College also took part in promoting The Cambridge School and the profession of landscape architecture. In 1934, the Trustees authorized the appointment of a landscape architect who would serve half-time on the faculty, strengthening the existing courses in Landscape Architecture, and spend the other half of his or her time redesigning the campus and supervising its maintenance. Dorothy May Anderson, then Co-director (with John Parker) of the Lowthorpe School in Groton, was chosen for the job and arrived in Northampton in 1935.[7] In time she became a well-rooted transplant. Serving under Professor Kate Reis Koch for teaching responsibilities and directly under President Neilson and the Board of Trustees for professional work on the campus comprised a fairly taxing schedule, but she managed to maintain a small private practice in Northampton quite apart from the college. Having a Cambridge School alumna on the faculty at Smith was an advantage during the period of affiliation, as she could interpret some of the unwritten rules and traditions of each institution to the other one. The long winter break between terms and the summer vacation at Smith made it possible for D. M. Anderson and Karl Putnam, the architect on the faculty, to teach short courses and serve as special critics at The Cambridge School.

Since the days of the Olmsted Plan, the campus had been disastrously neglected and encroached upon by all sorts of ill-thought-out conveniences of the moment. With few exceptions, the construction and planting required for revision of the campus was done by the Buildings and Grounds Staff. It was obvious that the success of any new plan by a landscape architect was very dependent on having a well-trained head gardener who could carry it out. At President Neilson's request, Miss Anderson looked for someone of the caliber of the earlier head gardeners — Canning, Downer, and Ellis — and she found him in New York on the roof of Rockefeller Center. W.I.P. Campbell, trained in horticulture at the Royal Botanical Garden in Edinburgh rather than at Kew, was the right man. When he came to Northampton for an interview with Mr. Neilson, the two Scots sealed the bargain with the alacrity of a highland fling and remained close friends throughout Mr. Neilson's lifetime.

Bill Campbell and D. M. Anderson worked well together in revising what was left of a campus plan and adjusting it to the requirements of new property and buildings as well as the ever-increasing number of bicycles that seemed to multiply faster than paths and racks could be supplied for them. The students were not particularly happy with any kind of rack. They would have preferred to ride their bikes into the classrooms and remain astride during a lecture, probably knitting Argyle sox throughout. Failing that, they usually settled for letting their bikes rest comfortably in grotesque piles on any patch of lawn that was reasonably near their classes. At that time, almost no autos were allowed on the campus, and the service roads were deliberately kept as narrow as possible. One of the most nightmarish and seemingly insoluble problems came not from the new buildings, which were outside the original campus area, but from a few obsolescent buildings that were definitely in the wrong places and blocked all coherent patterns of circulation in the middle of the campus. They served their purposes inefficiently, but as long as the roofs stayed on and water stayed out of the basements, the canny Scot President Neilson could not bring himself to have them torn down. Although Karl Putnam had no official responsibility for the campus and was a very busy man, he was generous in giving sound criticism of suggestions under consideration. In general design and interesting detail, the whole patchy assemblage of college properties was noticeably improved during the Anderson-Campbell-Putnam regime. Credit for the fact that at that time the campus was also beautifully maintained was due in large part to the well-trained staff, many of whom had come from England or Scotland.

Thoughts on the Past and the Future

Back in Cambridge, Henry A. Frost was philosophizing about

scholarships. In 1935, he wrote a fairly long statement for the *Alumnae Bulletin,* and because it is a commentary on attitudes prevailing in the 1930's, a few paragraphs are excerpted below:

"...There is a tendency to believe that a scholarship is a gift of tuition for which no one has paid and no one is expected to pay. It is not so simple as that.... If...income is less than operating expense...difficulties appear, which if they continue long enough will bring on an end to an institution's activities, however great its contribution to education.

"...[A scholarship is generally granted for one of three reasons.] It may be given to a brilliant student, without consideration of financial need.... It is...an honor to the individual which it is hoped will reflect prestige on the institution. A scholarship may be given with or without consideration of financial need [or brilliance] but for qualities of leadership.... The third type...goes to the student...who has shown himself [or herself] eager to learn, willing to make sacrifices, and in financial need. It goes to the plodder as often as to the genius.

"...Opinions differ as to the desirability of scholarships in any form in professional schools, and among those who approve in principle, there is a divergence of opinion as to the basis on which they should be granted. For many years The Cambridge School held firmly to the principle that scholarships should be granted only to the extent of funds already received.... During the past few years, for obvious reasons, our Council...has been more lenient and has permitted the granting of scholarships in anticipation of gifts. At no time, however, have our awards approached the proportion to whole tuition income...noted in undergraduate colleges."

Was this a worrisome premonition, perhaps recognition, of faint writing on the wall warning of the dangers of insolvency? He goes on to say:

"...I have never been able to justify the opinion sometimes held that no woman should undertake the professions... unless she has an independent income. I cannot imagine myself advising a young man of obvious intelligence against entering any profession simply because he is poor.... Nor can I advise women differently.... Success that comes from struggle is sweeter than success easily won. Failure after struggle is not dishonorable, and however discouraging, carries with it the satisfaction that one has given his (or her) best.... Study the lives of truly successful men and women. Where one succeeds, many must fail. This is also true of schools.... If our school is to be one of the few rising above the multitude..., you and I must have patience and a singleness of purpose, enduring not for a few years but for a lifetime. Schools are not made in a day nor in 20 years. Give us 50 years and let another generation judge us."

It had been twenty years since Henry Atherton Frost had somewhat reluctantly accepted his assignment to tutor a young lady who wanted to become a landscape architect, and some months after the statements quoted above, he reviewed the School's progress during that time. The geographic distribution of students was still surprisingly widespread for such a small school. Over a five-year period in the early 1930's, students came from twenty-one states and twenty-seven institutions. He noted that the 1933-34 registration was unusually large and that the 1934-35 registration was the smallest since 1923-24. Somewhere in the shadows Henrietta Cantabrigia was no doubt smiling her inscrutable feline smile and offering no explanation. The Director reminded his readers of the obvious truth that an adequately endowed school may ease along rather slowly through a critical period but that in an unendowed school "a crisis is immediately apparent, whether it results from weakness within the organization or from conditions...beyond its control, because such a school's activities are closely related to its earned income." He noted a gradual falling off in enrollment in all professional schools and attributed it, in part, to the fact that students who had already started their training when the Depression hit them somehow went on to finish. Those who had not yet started had second thoughts about the value of an expensive education in relation to its rewards. In another statement for the *Alumnae Bulletin* he says:

"Two facts have come to my attention lately.... A school of architecture which, in the past, has never had sufficient scholarships for promising students, this year (1935) has several desirable scholarships vacant because of a lack of eligible applicants. A department of [landscape] architecture in one of our largest universities, which has for years limited its registration of women to 10 percent of the student body, this year has an entering class one-third women, and a total registration one-quarter women. The department admits men who are [still] undergraduates... but women applicants must already hold a Bachelor's degree. These facts...are significant.... Fewer men are going into these two professions...[but] the number of women has not diminished."

For the first time, he discussed government projects as possible openings for graduating classes in both professions. Before, only private practice and the necessary apprenticeship leading to it had been considered. Both men and women were working on public projects, thought by some of the older professional men to be an eroding influence on the professions in general. In the somewhat ghostlike, perhaps ghastly, light of urban politics in the 1970's, one may ponder on the following comments made a quarter of a century ago.

> "As to the future, during the next 10-year period, it would seem suicidal for the federal, state, and city governments to sponsor large undertakings either in buildings or in landscape projects. In our cities and towns 'For Rent' signs on every hand lead us to expect little activity in the erection of office buildings, factories, warehouses, and stores. Business generally is in the doldrums. Undoubtedly, there will be repairs and modernization of existing buildings ...though one has but to study the financial conditions of churches, schools, theaters, clubs and similar organizations to expect little building activity in the near future from these sources."

At that time, housing held high priority among Henry Frost's many personal interests, and it is odd that he did not mention it here as a possible way out of the doldrums, but government-sponsored public housing projects had not yet appeared. Industrial parks and business offices in urban fringe areas were far in the future. The Director thought the period of tight money and a fairly dull future might be a disguised blessing for The Cambridge School. He said:

> "...many students with only a superficial interest in the two professions will be deterred from undertaking them.... Already the leaven is working.... The dilettante is disappearing.... We are confronted with an interesting paradox. As our earned income decreases, our teaching becomes more efficient because our material improves. We approach the millenium in the work for which the School is intended, while our necessary 'basis for continuity'...[fast disappears.]"

Only toward the end of his review of the first twenty years of The Cambridge School did Henry A. Frost launch into his favorite subject — housing. He thought it was the most promising field of the future and that his students would do well to enter this phase of activity. He says:

> "For generations, our housing, individually and collectively, has failed to keep pace with the development of other activities that make for human well-being. That we were the first school to give serious thought to the problem was chance, that we continued in this direction has been due to conviction, that we are in a favorable position for what has become a general and intense interest is due largely to our organization."

Henry A. Frost wanted to add housing as a fourth curriculum along with architecture, interior architecture, and landscape architecture. In June 1936 he proposed that The Cambridge School take over and continue the research bureau on housing that had been conducted by Albert Farwell Bemis. Mr. Bemis, a great friend of the School and a solid Rock of Gibraltar among its Trustees, had died very unexpectedly just a few months earlier. Everyone agreed with Mr. Frost, who in speaking of Mr. Bemis said that "the School owes much to his judgment, foresight, and generosity." Indeed it did. Any organization carrying on his work on housing, however, faced many obstacles. Several suggestions were made about how an activity that was basically research could be incorporated into The Cambridge School's training curricula, but no action was ever taken. Available records of 1936-38 activities are somewhat confusing, but it seems clear that President Neilson thought the widespread interest in housing probably was a temporary phenomenon, not deserving a separate emphasis, particularly when the matter of financing such a research bureau was very uncertain. The Executive Council was opposed to any plan that might increase expenses or complicate the financial situation of the School.[8]

Critical Times

The financial situation had become worse than ever, in fact precarious. The annual income simply wasn't large enough to cover taxes, rent, maintenance, and salaries, and no endowments were forthcoming. Mr. Frost, with Mr. Neilson's support, had appealed to the Carnegie Foundation [Corporation] for help. At that time, however, the policy of the Foundation was to consider only coeducational institutions as high priority, virtually the only priority. Since neither The Cambridge School nor Smith College could qualify on those grounds, their appeals for a generous grant to an endowment fund or even a smaller annual contribution of $5,000 were turned down.

The School had borrowed from its Trustee A. F. Bemis and from Smith College. The Bemis estate was in the process of settlement, and at one time it seemed as if the money The Cambridge School owed Mr. Bemis would have to be repaid to the estate immediately, even though the Bemis family staunchly supported the School. Mr. Neilson's loyalty to The Cambridge School never wavered, but he couldn't work miracles. The following excerpt from a letter he wrote to Mr. Frost at this time clearly shows his enormous good will, though one may question whether the business principles involved were as sound. He wrote:

"If it will save the School from having to pay the Bemis note [immediately] if Smith calls its loan a gift, I hereby call it a gift. . . . This letter may be taken as official, and I will get my action ratified at the next meeting of the Trustees."

Keeping track of the School's finances at any time required optimism and faith, but during the 1930's it must have seemed to those who tried to do so to have something in common with riding a roller coaster. As late as October 1937, the Director could report to the Trustees:

> "For the first time since this organization became definitely a school, the action of the. . .[Executive Council] makes it possible to offer for your acceptance an operating budget which not only is within our legitimate expected income but which contains provisions for some reduction of accumulated deficit. . . ."

By the spring of 1938, however, the situation had become so critical that the School had to be put on a sound financial base or go under completely. To become part of a larger institution, even if it meant sacrificing the complete independence so highly valued, seemed the only solution.

Though concerned with the need for financial security rather than academic degrees, the Great Dilemma of 1938 was much like the earlier one in 1928, chiefly because Radcliffe had once more come into the picture. President Conant had succeeded President Lowell at Harvard in 1933. He was more interested in The Cambridge School than President Lowell had been, and his attitude toward Radcliffe was very cooperative. Even though the membership of The Cambridge School Board of Trustees changed from time to time, there were always some Trustees who preferred a possible connection with Radcliffe to the existing one with Smith. By now the question was not one of affiliating an independent school with a prestigious college but rather one of incorporating a graduate school in dire financial need directly into the college structure. The choice had narrowed to Smith or Radcliffe. There was much to be said in favor of each, and much was said by members of the School's Executive Council, as well as by the Trustees of both Smith and The Cambridge School and by individuals at Harvard and Radcliffe.

The Board of Trustees of The Cambridge School, at a meeting on June 10, 1938, discussed the advantages of the two colleges in terms of general policy, academic attitudes, and experience in professional training. Radcliffe had had virtually no experience in teaching either architecture or landscape architecture, and it was the general understanding that a graduate school of Radcliffe would in fact be closely tied to the Harvard School of Design. Many of the group thought that in such an alliance The Cambridge School stood to lose much of its independent outlook. Bremer Pond, connected with both schools for so many years, said that "in a coeducational institution the general standards are never so good as in a school of one sex." Fletcher

Steele saw a significant advantage in a women's professional school being part of a women's college, and though this would have been true for Radcliffe as well as Smith, he thought The Cambridge School as part of Radcliffe would be "swallowed up" by Harvard. He doubted that a Harvard degree was worth it. Most of the Trustees felt that the danger of losing the School's unique character was greater if it became a part of Radcliffe than if it were an integral part of Smith. Radcliffe's chief advantage (considered by some to be a hazard) was, as always, its convenient location. One of the Trustees, Dean Hudnut of the Harvard School of Design, was not at the meeting, but he was fully aware of the matter under discussion.

Four graduates of The Cambridge School — Hope Slade Jansen, Amelia Peabody, Isabel DeCourcy Porter, and Eleanor Raymond — were on the Board of Trustees at the time. They favored a choice that would best assure independence of policy and action for the graduate school, and that pointed toward Smith. During the six years of affiliation, Smith College had given advice only when asked, and neither the College nor The Cambridge School had serious complaints about each other. All the Trustees, however, must have been aware of how much the success of the rather odd relationship depended upon William Allan Neilson and that he was about to retire.

In the end the decision was made not quite by the flip of a coin but more or less by the administrative procedures of the two colleges. President Comstock wanted to delay any decision until fall, when she and President Conant planned to review the entire question of graduate schools. Conversely, the officials at Smith College who would be responsible for adjusting the finances of any arrangement, wanted the matter to be decided immediately, or as soon as reasonably possible, in time for consideration in planning the budget.

So at the June 10 meeting it was voted unanimously (the member who also served on the Smith Board abstaining):

> "That the Board of Trustees of The Cambridge School of Architecture and Landscape Architecture petitions the Board of Trustees of Smith College to take over The Cambridge School as a Graduate School of Smith College, under the following terms and conditions:

> "The Cambridge School shall be clear of debt to the satisfaction of Smith College. The School property at 53 Church Street, Cambridge, shall be deeded to Smith College in trust on condition that Smith College shall carry on for ten years a Graduate School of Design, after which time said property shall become the property of the College without restrictions. The School shall give up all independence of organization and operation and equipment. Smith College shall appoint a Dean of the School, responsible directly to the President of the College; shall

regard instructors and professors appointed to the School as teaching appointments made by the College; shall appoint, if it seems desirable to the College, a member to their Board of Trustees who shall represent the interests of the School on that Board. The College shall permit, and so far as is reasonable, aid the School at such times as are proper, in the acquisition of endowment, scholarship and building funds, to the end that the School may become finally self-supporting."

Implementing the petition, another vote provided that "the Treasurer is hereby authorized to execute...any and all instruments...of said proposal...and deliver any agreements, stipulations, commitments, and deeds necessary to carry out fully the purport of the vote passed this day, on acceptance of Smith College." At the end of the meeting, all those present must have felt not exactly joyful but perhaps relieved that they had charted the course of their favorite school for at least the next ten years.

The Director of The Cambridge School was pleased with the decision of his Trustees and with that of the Trustees of Smith College, who almost immediately accepted the proposal to integrate the two institutions. He notified the alumnae formally through a letter in the *Alumnae Bulletin* for November 1938 stating his interpretation of the new arrangement and its value to The Cambridge School.[9] Hope Slade Jansen, President of the Alumnae Association, wrote a shorter but similar letter to the alumnae. She thought it a particularly happy coincidence that the incoming President of the Alumnae Association, Isabel DeCourcy Porter, was an alumna of Smith College as well as The Cambridge School. President Neilson wrote about the change of status as follows:

"Smith College, which has for some years been a sort of aunt to The Cambridge School, has now become its mother. It has taken this step because of the high value it places on the training given by the school and the record made by its graduates. It hopes that there will be no break in the admirable tradition of the school, and it welcomes its alumnae into the Smith College family with pride, and with confidence that the new relation will be of mutual benefit and to the advantage of the professions of architecture and landscape architecture."

The period of affiliation had ended, complete structural integration had begun. In December 1933, A. D. Taylor, then President of the American Society of Landscape Architects, wrote a long congratulatory letter to President Neilson, saying in part:

"...In this *Bulletin* [*Alumnae Bulletin of the Smith College Graduate School of Architecture and Landscape*

Architecture] I read with great interest and great satisfaction...of the adoption by Smith College of a new child from our growing family of landscape architects....

"There is great need for a school...having the backing and official recognition of a great women's college.... The Cambridge School should consider itself fortunate to be merged with an institution where its opportunities for future development and for service to the profession of landscape architecture may be so greatly increased. Women have a very important service to perform in the field of landscape architecture....

"Your great interest in our professional work...is greatly appreciated by the American Society of Landscape Architects...."

Members of the Smith College faculty who had followed the progress of The Cambridge School, particularly those involved in the interdepartmental major in architecture and landscape architecture, welcomed the new status of the graduate school. Its official position now was somewhat comparable to the widely known Smith College School for Social Work, which had been founded in 1918.

---

[1]See Appendix C for the full text of the proposal.

[2]The model was awarded the Gold Medal by the Massachusetts Horticultural Society at the Boston Spring Flower Show in 1935 and received several other high awards after that. An article about the project was published by PENCIL POINTS in November 1935.

[3]See Appendix D for the names of the candidates who received Master's degrees from Smith College in 1934 and 1935.

[4]One such college dropout, the author of this history, enrolled as an undergraduate at Smith College in 1940, making up the required science course she had skipped some twenty years before. She received her B.A. from Washington State University on the basis of transferred credits in 1941 and received an M.L.A. degree from Smith in 1942.

[5]Among the faithful volunteers at the Center were Edith Cochran, Margaret Clapp, Laura Cox, Priscilla Eddy, Elizabeth Clark Gunther, Dorothea Harrison, Priscilla Callan Houle, Grace Hight Kirkwood, Harriette Patey Long, Eleanor Lyman, Helen Norton, Frances Ward Olmsted, Georgia Hencken Perkins, Isabel DeCourcy Porter, Eleanor Raymond, Elizabeth Rice, Wenonah Sibley, Mary Nearing Spring, Anna Stearns, Nathalia Ulman, Muriel Childs Whitney, and Elizabeth Woolley.

[6]Itineraries for trips made in the mid-1930's are not available, but a later one is described by Mr. Frost in a letter to Mr. Davis in 1941: "I made two trips to Louisville — one round trip by car [probably the School stationwagon, with the exhibition], some 2,300 miles, and one trip...by car from which I returned by plane to keep my class appointments in Cambridge. The exhibition had a very good reception...by the local chapter of the American Institute of Architects. I gave three lectures: one to the architects, one at the University of Louisville, and one at the Louisville Collegiate School.... I then moved the exhibition to Oberlin and gave a lecture there.... I will return to Oberlin to dismantle the exhibition and had planned on bringing it directly to Cambridge.... [but] the University of Indiana has asked for it after...Oberlin. I am in some doubt, because of mileage and time limitations, whether we can accept that invitation, but I plan to...if it seems feasible. With all our activity it seems reasonably safe to say that the deficit for this year should not be greater than it was for last.... My

hope, of course, is that it may be less than last year. Obviously, I must raise a good deal of money for scholarships."

That same year he reported on the traveling exhibition being shown at Wellesley, Wheaton, Mt. Holyoke, and Vassar, and on requests that had been received from Sarah Lawrence, Goucher, Sweet Briar, and Georgia Tech. Although only men attended Georgia Tech, they wanted to see the show, too.

[7]The campus received a few surprises almost immediately. One excited student rushed in to tell her head-of-house that a tree, a BIG tree, was going right down Elm Street. "Well, don't worry about it dear," said Miss Denny, "either God or Miss Anderson will take care of it." Not everyone had such faith. The man who had charge of the grounds during part of the hodgepodge period was bitter about the presence of a landscape architect. Reportedly, he complained to President Neilson that she, among other misdemeanors, had taken half his job away from him. Mr. Neilson is said to have replied: "We're in the same boat. She's taken half of mine away, too."

[8]As it had from the very beginning, the Cambridge School continued to receive complaints about its name. About this time, Smith College objected to its unwieldly length and suggested that the official name be simplified to The Cambridge School. Mr. Frost reminded the College that another Cambridge School, a Day School for young children, predated the graduate school and was still functioning. He had promised not to duplicate its name officially, though unofficially his school was always The Cambridge School. He suggested, in connection with his proposal to add housing to the School's curricula, that the School's name be changed to The Bemis School. The Executive Council objected vehemently, saying that if any change were made in the name the School should become officially The Frost School. Until 1938 the name remained as cumbersome as ever — The Cambridge School of Architecture and Landscape Architecture: An Affiliated Graduate Professional School of Smith College. After 1938 it was The Smith College Graduate School of Architecture and Landscape Architecture: In Cambridge.

[9]See Appendix E.

Figure 6.1 — President and Mrs. William Allan Neilson at the doorway of their home on the Smith College campus. Both were interested in landscape architecture and were friends of The Cambridge School.

Figure 6.2 — The Hillyer Gallery, home of the Art Department in the 1930's. Some of the classes in architecture and landscape architecture were held here, others in Burton Hall. Hillyer also housed the office of the Resident Landscape Architect.

Figure 6.3 — Louise Leland, architect and efficient assistant to Henry A. Frost, just after receiving a master's degree in 1934 from her alma mater, Smith College.

Figure 6.4 — Eunice Garland (Hill) and Farnum Watkins were among the twenty-nine graduates of The Cambridge School who were granted Master of Landscape Architecture, M.L.A., degrees by Smith College in 1934.

Figure 6.5 — Scottish President Neilson tossing a spadeful of soil around the Scotch Elm planted in his honor in 1939. Looking on with Major Piper Ramsay are Scots W. I. P. Campbell, Head Gardener; Roderick A. MacLeod, tree surgeon; and William Sievwright, one of Smith's wizards with vines and shrubs.

Figure 6.6 — "Scale figure" Henry A. Frost on a house and garden trip in the 1930's.

Figure 6-7 — Mr. Frost discusses a fine point of brickwork with students in 1940.

Figure 6.8 — When the six-foot rule was missing, pacing the measurements was necessary.

Figure 6.9 — Cambridge School student on a house and garden trip to Newport, Rhode Island in the 1930's.

Figure 6.10 — Katharine Wilson (Rahn) and other Cambridge School students on the first trip to look at modern houses, about 1940. Kay now is an ASLA Fellow and maintains an active practice in Buffalo, New York.

Figure 6.11 — Miss Mary Gay and her water color class on a day when the weather was not good for painting outdoors.

Figure 6.12 — Ruth "Alabam" Smith (Bruckman) and her furry friend Max Willie in the backyard at 53 Church Street.

Figure 6.13 — Harriett Hasty (Gregg) and Hood's horse, claimed by many students in the late 1930's as a favorite pet. Harriett now practices landscape architecture in Florida.

Figure 6.14 — Cornelia Reck (Meiklejohn) while a student at The Cambridge School. After working for the Federal Government for a while, she developed a successful practice of her own in several parts of the country.

Figure 6.15 — Fleda Ochsner wearing her "cork & contour" hat made from discarded bits and pieces in the drafting room.

Figure 6.16 — WAVES training at Smith College in 1942. During World War II, Cambridge School women joined many branches of the military and intelligence services. They found their basic training adequate and reliable for the new challenges of cartography, camouflage, geographic model making, and emergency housing, especially for the shipyards.

Figure 6.17 — Cambridge School graduates Gertrude Sawyer and Dorothy May Anderson on the Smith campus in 1942. The Navy appreciatively accepted Miss Sawyer, who served in the WAVES throughout the war, but they rejected Miss Anderson, who then joined the Map Division of the OSS.

Figure 6.18 — For all Smith College alumnae, Paradise Pond is a memorable part of the campus. In this view, Mt. Tom appears in the distance.

7

Integration
1938-42

Though its everyday life remained about the same, the official status of The Cambridge School had changed considerably. It was not the free agent it had been, as it no longer held the deed to the property on Church Street and it no longer enjoyed complete independence of operation, which it had had under the affiliation of two autonomous institutions. Eleanor Raymond, who had known the School from the beginning, was named as a new member of the Smith College Board of Trustees to represent the interests of the Smith College Graduate School of Architecture and Landscape Architecture. During the period of affiliation the affairs of The Cambridge School had been mainly the responsibility of Board members Frank C. Smith of Worcester and Philip Hofer of Cambridge. Mr. Frost continued to explain to the alumnae the difference between affiliation and structural integration with Smith College, while the faculties of the undergraduate college and the graduate school worked to make the combined operation run smoothly.

The Alumnae Reeducated

Apparently, some of the alumnae of The Cambridge School did not entirely understand or approve of the basic change in the School's relationship to the College, in spite of the letter that Mr. Frost had written them shortly after the decision of June 10, 1938. They preferred affiliation to integration. They thought the earned reputation of The Cambridge School would disappear, or at least be eroded, by the change in the name of the school, which after many years was becoming well known. They wanted to know what would happen after the short 10-year period stipulated in the agreement. Would the graduate school be moved to Northampton? Because most of the alumnae had never been fully aware of the financial problems faced by the small school, they wanted to know why some solution could not be found that would preserve the autonomous status of The Cambridge School as they had known it.

In February 1939, Mr. Frost wrote the alumnae another letter saying that either they had not read his earlier one or that he had failed as a teacher to write a lucid report. He repeated in a one, two, three explanation that the changes were physical, economic, and educational. The building and its contents and the land at 53 Church Street had been transferred to Smith College, to be held in trust for ten years with the stipulation that the Graduate School be conducted in Cambridge during that period. After ten years the property would be owned by Smith, with no restrictions. As to the economic change, Mr. Frost explained that "...the Graduate School bears the same relation to the College as do other schools and departments....Thus our School has a definite basis of continuity and can plan its yearly program and its future with assurance...within the limits of the budget approved by the College." Educational changes, he assured the alumnae,were not great. He, the Director, would still be responsible for policy and conduct of the Graduate School. Instead of reporting to a Cambridge School Board of Trustees as he had done before, he would report directly to the President of Smith College. He encouraged the widely scattered alumnae, many of whom were also Smith alumnae, to join the Smith Club nearest them.

Smith College took over the Scholarship Fund and added one full scholarship, $1,000, to it. Mr. Frost challenged The Cambridge School Alumnae Association to raise $2,000 for the Fund's use in 1939-40. The Scholarship Committees of the College and the Graduate School were closely coordinated, but points of view among the members were not always identical. With rare exceptions, The Cambridge School had always opposed granting a full-tuition scholarship to an entering first-year student, preferring to wait until she proved her worth and then increasing the stipend according to the need (or as long as the money held out). Conversely, the College considered a scholarship as a reward for outstanding work already accomplished and wanted to grant a full scholarship for one year only. The recipient could fend for herself after that. The actual compromise plan was a bit spotty, having elements of both approaches.

Adjustments on All Fronts

After 1938, a somewhat closer bond between the faculties of the two groups was noticeable. Professors from the Art Department at Smith gave special lectures in Cambridge, and their counterparts there lectured to the undergraduates in Northampton. Mr. Frost, however, did not approve a suggestion that professors be exchanged on a semester or full-year basis. He cherished his policy of continuity in teaching, with an occasional outsider to liven up the classes with a fresh point of view, and he also knew that he had no control over the schedules set by the Harvard School of Design for the men on its faculty who also taught at The Cambridge School.

In the mid-1930's, during the period of affiliation, Mr. Frost had proposed separating the combined courses in the Art and Botany Departments at Smith into majors in Architecture and in Landscape Architecture, both in the Art Department. His hope was that a student who had finished an undergraduate major in either field could come into The Cambridge School with advanced standing and finish the graduate course in two and a half instead of three and a half years. The proposal was not enthusiastically received by members of the Smith faculty who had worked hard to integrate the two fields through an interdepartmental approach. With the advantage of hindsight, it seems strange that the life-long advocate of a close relationship between the two professions could not have accepted the interdepartmental major as it was and considered it basic to either curriculum in the graduate school. Perhaps he was mired in the detail of too many plans and proposals. One such that came to naught but is interesting to look back on was that Smith should arrange a Junior Year at The Cambridge School similar to the Junior Year Abroad in the field of languages. This was a swing of 180 degrees from President Neilson's suggestion in 1928 that the first year of graduate training be offered in Northampton, not Cambridge.

From time to time, faculty members and students alike questioned the granting of Bachelor's degrees in Architecture and Landscape Architecture to candidates from the Graduate School. The Cambridge School had been influenced by a general wave of reorganization of architectural schools during the mid-1930's, when Columbia, Princeton, and M.I.T., among others, had revised requirements for degrees in Architecture, and the School of Design at Harvard was planning to grant a Bachelor's degree in Architecture for the work that before had led to a Master's degree and to require work beyond the new B.Arch. to receive an M.Arch. degree. During the period of affiliation, Smith College had somewhat reluctantly approved the granting of a B.Arch. and a B.L.A., as well as the M.Arch. and M.L.A., but the relationship between them seemed hazy. Primarily, the plan was to offer a higher level of training toward the Master's degree while shortening the time in Graduate School for some students by recognizing acceptable undergraduate work. To many it was a confusing concept. The Director explained it thus:

"... Bachelor of Architecture and Bachelor of Landscape

Architecture...are graduate degrees. The requirements are first a B.A. degree from a recognized institution, followed by a professional course similar to that now offered for the degrees of M.Arch. and M.L.A. The Master's degrees will then be given for more advanced work of a different nature than now offered....Actually, ...little more time will be required than is now necessary for the [Master's] degrees.

"...In the past, undergraduate technical schools have been handicapped by the immaturity of students in the more advanced professional subjects, while the graduate technical schools have found the college graduates perhaps too mature for their more elementary technical courses which may require...hours of patient drudgery, because their purpose is to train the hand and eye quite as much as the mind. Thus a more elastic educational policy which permits a student to lay the foundations of her professional career early in her school course, and to carry on the more advanced technical studies when she is more mature, has distinct advantages and should be encouraged."

The students affected felt that actually about as much work was required for a Bachelor's as for a Master's degree, and they tended to continue until they qualified for the latter. The B.Arch. and B.L.A. program was never widely or clearly understood, and very few Bachelor's degrees in either field were ever granted by Smith. A suggestion that The Cambridge School itself enhance the recognition given non-college students by granting them Bachelor's and Master's Certificates was vetoed by Majorie Nicolson, Academic Dean of Smith College, who quite rightly thought that such a practice would tend to compound an already confusing situation.

At first, the annual budget and the assignment of specific courses in the Graduate School caused some difficulty. The College Treasurer customarily received proposed budgets in January. The Cambridge School (officially the Smith College Graduate School with the long name but still referred to as The Cambridge School) found a January deadline hard to meet. Most of its faculty members had higher priority commitments to the Harvard School of Design, and they didn't know until later in the year what their teaching load might be. Thus, it was not easy to estimate the cost of specific courses and total outlay for salaries so early in the year. The Treasurer considered the new Graduate school to be a problem child that must eventually be brought into line and was not entirely willing to accept faith in the future as a basis for expenditures. Among other requests for clarification of budget items he asked for justification of what he considered to be exhorbitantly high bills for electricity. President Neilson knew that the students in Cambridge worked in both drafting rooms until midnight every night, and shortly before his retirement he seems to have intervened in the electric-bill controversy, saying in a letter to Mr. Frost, "I think that at present the extra cost of electric light and heat will not be enough to justify curbing the enthusiasm of the students." He went on to say that if the bills got to be too high, something could be done about it later on. And so things went along during a period of more or less continuous adjustment on all fronts.

Shortly after the first year of The Cambridge School's integration with Smith College, almost 25 years since its founding, Mr. Frost reported to the alumnae thus:

> "For those of us who teach, the New Year dates not from January first...but from a Monday late in September. By January we are nearly half through the academic year and perilously near disillusionment on our [September] resolutions. This report...marks a quarter-century for the School.... When the affair started we were all very young, and...we are still surprisingly young for what may seem to many of you our extremely advanced years.

> "...Our School started in the midst of a world war. It has grown up during a period of economic uncertainty and social unrest. It enters its second quarter-century on the eve of another war, which if allowed to run its course, may work destruction greater than we dare to contemplate. ...All of us hope...that future generations may be more intelligent in their use of the gifts of civilization.

> "...Our major problem is no longer primarily the size of next year's entering class or next month's salary list. We are looking further into the future, attempting to visualize conditions as they may be after this maelstrom is over, trying to be more intelligent in order that our students may go out not merely with a cargo of knowledge but also with a supercargo of intelligence, so vastly more important than knowledge...."

Considering the tense state of Europe in the summer of 1939, just before Hitler's armies marched into Poland, it was certainly optimistic of The Cambridge School to plan two European Travel Courses — one to Italy and the other to Scandinavia. Though administrative details had not been worked out entirely during the spring, the possibility of giving course credit to students from Harvard and Radcliffe who wanted to join the group was being considered. It is doubtful that the 1939 study trips abroad went beyond the early planning stage, as they are not mentioned in available reports for the rest of the year.

The Interim Presidency

Midst much fanfare, William Allan Neilson retired from the

presidency of Smith College in 1939, after twenty-two years of truly distinguished service. His last official act was conferring an Honorary Degree upon his wife, Elizabeth Muser Neilson, whose enthusiasm for good architecture and good landscape design matched his own. Mr. Neilson spoke of the incident as "the most delicate and embarrassing task the trustees ever laid upon me." Mrs. Dwight W. Morrow, who had been president of the Alumnae Association when President Neilson took office in 1917, became an interim President of Smith while the College continued its search for a new president. Mr.Neilson was so widely recognized as the soul and spirit of Smith College that, in the current slang, his was a hard act to follow.

Having Elizabeth C. Morrow as President of Smith was neither an advantage nor a disadvantage to the new graduate school in Cambridge. She was well liked, and in her job of holding the whole complex college together until a more permanent president could take over, she was an able administrator. However, the tradition of having a man as President of Smith was very deeply rooted throughout the College and the Alumnae Association, and there was never any thought of Mrs. Morrow's serving longer than the time needed to find the right man for the position. It was generally said that Smith, unlike other women's colleges, would never have a woman president. Obviously, this stubborn prejudice had been laid to rest by 1975, when Jill Ker Conway became Smith's seventh president.

The most outstanding achievement of The Cambridge School in public relations during Mrs. Morrow's presidency was an exhibition on "Houses and Housing" at the Somerset Hotel in Boston. It was an excellent show originally prepared by the Museum of Modern Art in New York to which examples of work by members of The Cambridge School Faculty were added. The exhibition was well attended as were two lectures, one on "Experiences in Modern Architecture," by Mrs. Walter Gropius and the other on "Modern Trends in Landscape Architecture," by Cynthia Wiley, an alumna then practicing in New York. Judging by the prestigious list of Honorary Sponsors, the School had indeed finally achieved solid recognition[1]. Behind the scenes, the Alumnae Association, under the chairmanship of Isabel Porter, contributed hours of hard work on all the chores, expected and unexpected, that preceded the opening on February 29th.

In the summer of 1940 the Smith College Graduate School of Architecture and Landscape Architecture and the Harvard Graduate School of Design collaborated for the first time on one summer school for both. The Collaborative Summer School was announced by a very handsome folder sent out to colleges throughout the country for posting on bulletin boards. Walter F. Bogner, Christopher Tunnard, Carol Fulkerson, and Albert E. Simonson comprised its faculty. They assigned the full six-week period to a problem of land subdivision that involved both disciplines, and everyone seemed pleased with the results. Of the fifty students enrolled, twenty were women, fifteen of them from The Cambridge School.

Though in 1928 it had seemed a circumstance most unlikely to occur again, by 1938 the School was once more running out of space. Not only were there more students, but the cumbersome models, used to such great advantage in teaching and for exhibition, encroached on the drafting rooms. Plans for a new building with full-lot frontage on Church Street, a two-story building designed by the Cambridge School faculty, were presented to the alumnae in May 1939. The building was to include lecture rooms, instructor's offices, and a drafting room large enough to accommodate seventy-seven tables. The downstairs drafting room in the existing building (rapidly coming to be considered as the "old" building, even though recent coats of white paint and a bright red stair rail had dressed it up remarkably) was to be converted into a studio, and the upstairs drafting room was to accommodate the library and study rooms.

Predictably, The Cambridge School was more enthusiastic about the plans than was the Smith College Board of Trustees, which turned down an appeal for funds early in 1940. Mrs. Morrow wrote Mr. Frost that although the Trustees were not willing to finance the building, he should feel free to raise whatever money he could through private gifts (EXCEPT from the Smith College alumnae, who were then in the midst of a drive toward a very large Alumnae Fund). She added that despite their turning down the building plan, the Trustees had voted another $600 scholarship for the Graduate School. Even though the Trustees obviously and logically did not want to approve any new building plans during the term of an interim president, they might well have been no more enthusiastic under normal circumstances, as their interest had always been focused on urgent needs in Northampton. By the end of 1940, Mr. Frost had scaled down the building plans to a series of small additions to the drafting-room wings, units which could be added gradually over a period of years. Apart from financial reasons, the less ambitious plan seemed more desirable to some because it did not sacrifice the old Dalby House, which many thought of as the core of The Cambridge School.

New President of Smith

On October 17, 1940, Herbert John Davis, formerly Chairman of the English Department at Cornell University, was inaugurated as President of Smith College. Even before the inauguration, Mr. Frost had written a long letter to Mr. Davis summarizing the history of The Cambridge School and setting forth its goals and problems, at that time mostly problems.[2] On October 11, he wrote another letter outlining the general expenses of the School for the past five years and enclosing tables that covered a longer period — 1924-1940.[3]

Publicity about the School had not received as much attention during the last years of affiliation as it had earlier. Efforts had been relaxed, in part, on the assumption that the prestige and favorable public relations of Smith College itself would carry over to the Graduate School. Ironically, the reverse was true. The Cambridge School had become fairly well known under that name, and the overly long titles of the School as an affiliate of Smith College and later as one of its graduate schools tended to confuse rather than clarify. The School lost part of its identity when its official name was changed, and in spite of all attempts to keep "Cambridge" prominently in the title, many people thought of the Smith College Graduate School of Architecture and Landscape Architecture as being part of the College in Northampton. In their minds they did not associate it with the small but excellent school they had known, or had heard of, in Cambridge. Therefore, as soon as President Davis took office, Mr. Frost proposed reinstating The Cambridge School Traveling Exhibition, and much of their early correspondence was about suitable methods of transporting such an exhibition. The Trustees were concerned about the cost of such a public relations venture, as perhaps from their point of view it seemed an irrelevant adventure. From the beginning, however, Mr. Davis was enthusiastic about the show and wanted to put it on the road and keep it there. Thus the year 1940 ended, with the two men exchanging cordial notes while feeling their way rather cautiously through circumstances new to both of them.

The Year 1941

The first full year of President Davis's administration was such a strangely euphoric one for The Cambridge School that it deserves special attention. The tone of all the correspondence both in and out of The Cambridge School that year was optimistic and forward looking, though the specter of the seemingly irreducible deficit persisted in the shadows.

An entirely new collection of drawings, photographs, and models had been assembled for the Traveling Exhibition. In January, plans for showing it through the help of Smith Alumnae Clubs were completed, after it was made clear to the Smith women that the show was intended for publicity, not as a competitive attempt to raise funds. Before this innovative plan went into effect, the exhibition had been shown only at colleges. Now it was possible to reach a larger number of women who might be interested in architecture and landscape architecture, and the Traveling Exhibition again became a major undertaking.

The March issue of *The Cambridge School Alumnae Bulletin* reflected a change of emphasis from the mid-1930's, though its general approach was still one of looking forward for more worlds to conquer.

Jobs in relation to our aid to Britain during 1941 were gradually replacing the public works and other government jobs of the Depression days, and several Cambridge School women were taking part in these early war efforts, particularly near the shipyards. Although many graduates were forming professional partnerships among themselves, usually but not always an architect and a landscape architect, the shift away from private estates and toward larger-scale work was noticeable. Public housing was receiving much attention.

Perhaps reliving the experiences of the World War I period, Mr. Frost wrote to the alumnae thus:

> "...That the war will end is certain, if only from the exhaustion of the belligerents. That the burden of rehabilitation will be heavy upon us all, and that there will be tremendous need for intelligent thought and action, can be accepted without argument.... There is much unrest among students, which is reflected in us who are older, or perhaps the unrest was ours first and theirs in reflection. ...If we are to retain our sanity in an insane world, it is essential that we carry on without interruption the normal pursuits of life, but if we see further than that, to a time when exhausted people may look to us for help in reestablishing a crumbling civilization, we must realize that this is no time for uncertainty or hesitation. For us these are years of great opportunity. We must think clearly, act courageously, plan boldly...."

During the spring, ties between the Art Department and the Graduate School were tightened in various ways. Karl Putnam planned to spend all or most of his forthcoming sabbatical leave teaching in the Graduate School in Cambridge. In exchange, Si Simonson was to spend the semester in Northampton, but because of later complications it was Miss Anderson who took over Mr. Putnam's classes. Mr. Frost, thinking of the additional advanced work he had recommended for students who received a Bachelor's degree and wanted to continue until they qualified for a Master's, suggested a new program, which for want of a better term he called "socialized architecture". One marvels at his temerity, as the term itself was bound to strike the persons who held the purse strings as somewhat visionary, to say nothing of the fact that he needed more space and more money to make the proposal a reality.

On June 20, he wrote a long letter to President Davis in which he discussed his plan for advanced training and the need for more definite guidelines from the administration. He called attention particularly to how few years had elapsed since it was generally agreed that "a woman's place is in the home," and noted the progress women had made recently and the fact that their work had become much more widely recognized. He thought such recognition was overdue, and undoubtedly having his own alumnae collectively in mind, he spoke of a woman as one who

"...thinks clearly, reasons well, and is interested in housing rather than houses; in community centers for the masses rather than in neighborhood clubs for the elite; in regional planning more than in estate planning; in the social aspects of her profession more than in private commissions. In the field of research she is thorough. In the adaptation of this research to the requirements of everyday problems she is intelligent. She coordinates her work well, collaborates with others successfully. Her horizon has broadened steadily in these past ten years...."

Although his appraisal did not entirely fit all individuals among the alumnae, as many were still more interested in private than in public work, it did indicate new attitudes and a gradual opening of more doors for professional women.

An Alumnae Conference, patterned to some extent on the Smith Alumnae College but in part an outgrowth of the traditional Cambridge School Alumnae Day, was held at the School in June. The ten women who attended pronounced the going-back-to-school week a stimulating experience.

The search for endowment and scholarship funds continued, and during the summer of 1941, President Davis, on behalf of the Graduate School, appealed to the Rockefeller Foundation. Scholarships were badly needed, and once again the answer was disappointing and also frustrating, because it seemed so likely to be "yes" but was actually "no". In a letter to President Davis, Dr. Raymond B. Fosdick said:

"I have had an opportunity to read Mr. Frost's report on the School of Architecture (sic) in Cambridge. I had not realized...that the institution was twenty-six years old. Frost's plans seemed to us to be well conceived, and I have ...discussed them with some of my associates here. Unfortunately, the Foundation has never gone into this kind of work, and it lies outside the periphery of any activities which the Trustees have thus far authorized. I would not want to say that this is a final answer, because to argue that what has never been done can never be done is poor reasoning. But emergencies which now confront the world are bringing increasing pressure on us for financial assistance in realms of scholarship which we have already supported, and my own belief is that the Trustees would be reluctant to go into a new field at this time."

During the fall, the students were coping with new assignments. Some of them had attended the second Collaborative Summer School of the Smith College Graduate School and the Harvard School of Design. They and others were taking an active part in a recently formed discussion group that included members from Harvard and M.I.T. as well as The Cambridge School. Aside from exchanging ideas, these students were trying out their wings by publishing a new magazine. *TASK*.

The enrollment in 1940 had been down slightly, but in September 1941, forty-nine students arrived from eighteen different colleges and schools, and two or three more were expected. Mr. Frost's earlier pleas for more space had been ignored by the College administrative offices, but the situation now was critical, and two fairly large offices in the Sage Building across the street from the School were rented for $100 a month. President Davis sent a congratulatory note about the high enrollment, which he attributed chiefly to the success of the publicity the Traveling Exhibition engendered. He added that he hoped the expenses of the extra rooms could be mostly covered by the additional income from tuition.

On October 9, Mr. Frost reported on income and expenditures for the month of September 1941, as compared to September 1940, and discussed estimates and tentative scheduling of the Traveling Exhibition for the Spring of 1942.[4] He also commented on the Smith Plan, which was "coming along in a very interesting manner," despite the fact that he hadn't yet received the topographical survey. This comment needs an explanation.

From the time of his arrival in Northampton the year before, President Davis had wanted to establish a firm base for logical expansion of the College. He was not particularly interested in retaining a resident landscape architect who had made some significant improvements to the campus but who could do little more than revise earlier plans and keep the place in good running order. He thought that if one architect on the faculty was sufficient, it was quite unnecessary to have two landscape architects, Miss Koch and Miss Anderson. He wanted one big comprehensive plan for buildings and grounds that would be flexible enough to accommodate new buildings in the foreseeable future, meaning the next twenty-five years, and yet firm enough to let him avoid making bothersome decisions. He could simply say, "Look at The Plan." It seemed a very sound idea, though colleges are not noted for growing along logical lines. He sought Mr. Frost's advice, and as a result The Plan for Smith College came into existence.

Both men were extremely enthusiastic about such a plan, because it was to serve as a teaching tool while in the making, keep faculty members in both the College and the Graduate School well occupied (as though they hadn't been before), and furnish for once and for all a sound quarter-century site plan for new buildings. President Davis asked Miss Anderson to have a comprehensive topographic survey made during the late summer, Mr. Simonson and Mr. Fulkerson were put in charge of both the teaching aspect of the project and its ultimate completion for utilitarian purposes, Miss Raymond was called in as an advisor and a link with the Trustees, and a special grant of $1,000 was made toward anticipated expenses of the project. Obviously having received the missing survey by November 25, Mr. Frost reported then that significant progress had been made on three topographic models: 1) the campus as it was in 1875; 2) the present campus (1941); and 3) the quarter-century plan for future expansion (1966). President Davis was delighted, and the "committee" of Simonson, Fulkerson, Raymond, Putnam and Anderson had all they could do to keep up with the students and to approve or disapprove suggestions that came in from all quarters. (Today's students and visitors to Smith College can thank them for disapproving a proposed large addition to the Dean's house, which would have blocked the view of Paradise Pond.)

Almost hidden in a letter written by President Davis to Mr. Frost on November 28, 1941, only three days after Mr. Frost's report on the satisfactory progress of the Smith Plan, was a sentence indicating trouble ahead, but since the warning was incidental to a discussion of several other topics, the seriousness of the situation was not immediately apparent. Apropos of expenses of the Graduate School, President Davis said:

> "I am much afraid that unless we can substantially reduce the present deficit the Trustees will decide to give up the school at the earliest possible moment, and I think you ought to know of this danger and take it into account in connection with all proposals for added expenses."

This was a word to the wise about a budget that was due in January. In the same letter, President Davis also commented on the likelihood of having to run the Smith College School for Social Work at a deficit in the future[5].

The first issue of the 1941-42 *Alumnae Bulletin* was circulated about the first of December. In his customary letter to the alumnae, Mr. Frost discussed the activities of the past year and plans for the future. On the subject of the Traveling Exhibition, he remarked that he and Mr. Geary would make a real addition to a Barnum and Bailey roustabout crew or to any of the Army's transportation units. As to rewards for their labor, his wry appraisal of the situation was not unlike that made after a speaking tour in the 1920's, when he thought the School might have been better off if he had stayed by his own fireside. He now said:

> ". . . Last year the new President, Mr. Davis, supported our publicity campaign generously, and, as some of you know,

we exhibited in several colleges and other centers. But now comes the strange part of the story. With a bumper enrollment of new students, which we perhaps have a right to think is owing to publicity, not one of these students comes to us directly from an institution at which we showed our work last year, except Smith College. The implication is that when enough time has elapsed so that we have been able to show our exhibition at all the educational institutions attended by women in this country, our registration will go down to zero. While I am not positive of this, I think that all publicity must be regarded as secondary rather than primary in its effect...."

In general, in early December 1941, things were going smoothly at The Cambridge School for faculty, alumnae, and students alike. Then came the Japanese attack on Pearl Harbor and its traumatic aftermath. No one thought of much else during the rest of that year.

---

[1] The Honorary Sponsors included many who were associated with Harvard — Professors Joseph Hudnut, George H. Edgell, Walter Gropius, Paul J. Sachs, Henry V. Hubbard, Philip Hofer, Kenneth John Conant, Arthur Pope and their wives, and Bremer W. Pond, then Head of the Department of Landscape Architecture in the Graduate School of Design. Also included were Dean *emeritus* William Emerson and Dean Walter Cornack of the Massachusetts Institute of Technology and their wives, Presidents Ada Louise Comstock of Radcliffe and Mildred McAfee of Wellesley, and from the Smith College Board of Trustees, Mr. Frank C. Smith and his wife and Miss Eleanor Raymond.

[2] See Appendix F.

[3] See Appendix G.

[4] See Appendix H.

[5] See Appendix I.

8

An End and a Beginning
1942

Among the first institutions to be affected by World War II were colleges and graduate schools. Throughout the 1930's, faculty members and administrative officers had been aware of the political and military situation in Europe, particularly those in institutions along the eastern seaboard. Although the many intellectual refugees who somehow escaped and came instinctively to American colleges told frightening stories of what was going on in their homelands, their more fortunate colleagues in this country had become not exactly inured but at least very used to an atmosphere of concern and pending crisis. Immediately after Pearl Harbor, however, students and young faculty members began dropping out to join the military services or to take war jobs that sprang up almost overnight. Harvard was not immune to the problems created by the general exodus. Men were leaving in greater numbers every day, and as no one knew how long the war might go on, the university administrators could foresee a potentially serious drain on financial resources. The possibility of admitting women to the Harvard graduate schools had been discussed by the faculty off and on for several years, ever since President Conant brought a more liberal outlook to the university, but before Pearl Harbor little progress had been made toward a goal that was not widely favored. When enrollment figures looked very uncertain, such discussions were intensified, though they still took place behind the scenes and in guarded terms.

An Unexpected Crisis

In the early part of 1942, Smith College and its graduate school in Cambridge seemed generally unaffected by the atmosphere of crisis.

To visitors and students all appeared to be relatively calm on the campus in Northampton. Special wartime courses in map reading and drafting had not yet been set up by the Army, and the Navy had not yet decided to use Smith College as one of its main training centers for the WAVES. In Cambridge, the faculty and students in the Graduate School were working night and day on the long-range plan for the college campus. Underneath it all, however, everyone felt uncertain about the future in general and worried about how it might affect his or her life personally. Throughout the country, persons with authority were putting into effect rather short-sighted policies on many different fronts. Whether the Trustees and administrative officers of Smith College fell into this category and reflected the jittery mood of the times as they considered the possibility of closing The Cambridge School, or whether they sincerely thought such a move would be beneficial to all concerned, is even today a matter of personal opinion.[1]

Behind the scenes, things were far from calm. At their regular fall meeting in October 1941 the Smith College Trustees had discussed many things, including the folly of running graduate schools at a deficit. The matter of trimming expenses of The Cambridge School had been discussed before and was discussed then in an appeal for a greatly reduced budget for the next year. In his letter to Mr. Frost of November 28, President Davis had warned him that if the current deficit and the new budget were not reduced there was danger of a seriously negative reaction on the part of the Trustees. (See Chapter VII. Appendix I.) Most of the letter, however, concerned the progress of The Plan for Smith College. So on December 30, Mr. Frost went to Northampton to talk to President Davis about The Plan, general affairs in Cambridge, the upcoming annual budget, and the Trustees' attitude toward The Cambridge School.

One can only guess Mr. Frost's reaction when he found that the situation was much more serious than he had thought. It was not just a matter of cutting the budget down to the bone and later discussing the possibility of giving up the Graduate School sometime in the future, presumably at the end of the ten-year trial period agreed upon in 1938, if the financial situation did not improve. The Trustees were not thinking of future possibilities but of actually closing the Graduate School almost immediately. Mr. Frost realized for the first time that a break with Smith College was not just possible but was imminent and that there was to be no discussion whatever of alternatives nor of the long-range advantages and disadvantages of maintaining The Cambridge School. The future value of a well-established, top-ranking professional graduate school for women as part of a women's college was not to be considered. The decision was to be made on the basis of deficit alone. Considering the importance of projects in process, it seemed a most illogical proposal. Whether the conversation between the two men ended with an option or an ultimatum is moot. If there was a choice, it was that the Graduate School could continue *if* it raised all the money necessary to run it, with no help from general college funds. Under the circumstances, such an option was virtually an ultimatum.

Mr. Frost returned to Cambridge and quietly discussed the critical situation with his faculty. These teachers were surprised, as they considered closing the Graduate School to be a violation not only of the spirit but also of the letter of the June 10, 1938 proposal for integration, which had been accepted by the College. (See Chapter VI.) They recalled the sentence that read: "The School property at 53 Church Street, Cambridge, shall be deeded to Smith College in trust on condition that Smith College shall carry on for ten years a Graduate School of Design, after which time said property shall become the property of The College without restriction." Perhaps no one remembered the next sentence, which read: "The School shall give up all independence of organization and operation and equipment." Complying with the terms of this same agreement, The Cambridge School had cleared away all debts before becoming an integral part of the College in 1938, but during the following four years it had accumulated a sizable deficit. In normal times, many problems might have been solved to everyone's satisfaction. At least, some time would have been devoted to discussing alternatives. But these were not normal times, and as has been said of many another situation, all's fair in love and war. This was wartime, less than a month after Pearl Harbor.

The Director of The Cambridge School and its faculty concluded that it would be financially impossible to operate their favorite school as an entirely independent institution, even if some arrangement other than the one with Smith could be found to solve the problem of granting degrees. Nor could the Graduate School survive as part of Smith if it had to pay all the bills. The whole picture had changed since the break-even days of the 1920's, before the market crash of 1929. The crash and the depression that followed it dried up several potential sources of large endowment gifts to The Cambridge School, and although the enrollment tended to increase, tuition income could never cover the greatly increased costs of teaching, publicity, and maintenance. In 1942, no friend arrived in court to defend the work of The Graduate School or to offer a viable alternative to the arrangement then in operation.

Smith Trustees Vote to Close the Graduate School

The two sides viewed the tunnel from different points of view, but the small light both saw at the end was the likelihood that the Harvard

Graduate School of Design would soon admit women. When it became clear to all that The Cambridge School would have to close, things happened rapidly. Mr. Frost reported to President Davis on the meeting with his faculty, and on January 14, President Davis, perhaps with the Treasurer looking over his shoulder, wrote a letter to the Trustees asking for a postal vote on whether to close the Graduate School in Cambridge.[2] Presenting operating deficits and other pertinent information from the Treasurer's office, he asked to be empowered to act immediately. In part, he wrote:

> "I am writing to ask whether you approve of this, although it would entail the return of the land and building at 53 Church Street to its donor, Mrs. Faith B. Meem, and the return of the scholarship fund to Mrs. Hurlbut. Would you also be willing to give me power to act and to refer the details to the Committee on Finance and Investment to be settled at their meeting on January 23rd."

The hand of the Treasurer was evident throughout the letter, although President Davis added that both Mr. Frost and Mr. Neilson approved the proposal and advised closing the school at the end of the academic year. This was literally true, as faced with the unfavorable financial situation and the great uncertainty of the immediate future, these two men dwelt on the likelihood that Harvard (still spoken of in all correspondence as "a neighboring institution") would decide to admit women, and they spoke of the many years it had taken to achieve this general goal. Privately, however, the dreams of an equal but separate opportunity for women to receive excellent training in the two professions in which these two men were particularly interested were flattened as effectively as though run over by a bulldozer. It was the end of Mr. Frost's plans for an outstanding graduate school for women, not coeducational, which he had thought could be built up as part of a women's college. It was also the end of Mr. Neilson's dreams of an active graduate school that would enhance the prestige of Smith College. Both made the most of it and publicly stressed the advantages of a possible new era at Harvard, though at that time the behind-the-scenes discussions about admitting women to the Harvard graduate schools focused on such a move being temporary and were usually qualified by the phrase "for the duration of the war."

The Trustees' votes that came in by mail shortly after January 14 were almost unanimous in favor of closing The Cambridge School. Only Eleanor Raymond voted "no". Accompanying letters from many Trustees indicated that their votes were cast solely on the need to cut costs in every way possible, and if this was one way, they were all for it.

The Chess Game

Smith, Harvard, and The Cambridge School had agreed to keep all discussions of the pending three-way action confidential. The timing of a necessary announcement, a factor that had always affected the affairs of The Cambridge School, now became extremely important. Toward the end of January the situation must have seemed somewhat like a three-cornered chess game. At Smith the matter was settled. The Trustees had voted, and on January 23 the Committee on Finance and Investment had considered the details of closing the Graduate School. The next regular meeting of the Smith Board was set for February 20, when the postal vote would undoubtedly be ratified. At Harvard, however, the next regular meeting of the Board of Overseers was scheduled for March 2, and it was expected that at that time Harvard would announce a new policy of admitting women, under certain specified conditions. The details of how such a policy would affect the Graduate School of Design were still uncertain. As the third player in the game, The Cambridge School was checkmated. Inevitably, rumors of the School's closing were spreading, and Mr. Frost feared that his students might hear of it from someone on the outside. He had agreed not to say anything about pending changes until after Harvard announced that it would admit women. A few personal conversations and phone calls brought things to a head.

On February 3, the Harvard Board of Overseers held a special meeting. They voted that "upon the recommendation of the Faculty of Design, for the duration of the war, women would be admitted to the Graduate School of Design as candidates for its degrees, upon the same terms as those applied to men." The Faculty of Design had so recommended in January. Dean Hudnut had not wanted to include the phrase "for the duration of the war," as he believed that the move should be and would be permanent, but he approved the wording of the proposal to assure passage. Professor Gropius wanted women admitted to the School of Design as special students, not as candidates for degrees. Since he was one of the instigators for admitting women to Harvard, his attitude in this case was surprising, but, apparently, he was reconciled to the wording of the vote as passed. The hapless pawns in the game were the few students who held no Bachelor's degree and were working toward Cambridge School Certificates. They were not eligible to enter Harvard's School of Design or any other graduate school, though at that time the requirements for a Certificate and a Bachelor's degree were identical. Therefore, Mr. Frost arranged to have Smith grant Bachelor's degrees to those students who normally would have been granted Cambridge School Certificates in June 1942 (or at a later date if they had fulfilled all the requirements).

On the morning of February 4, with no advance warning to the students but with the informal approval of President Davis, Mr. Frost posted the following notice on the bulletin board.

To the Students:

This is to inform you of three recent decisions of Harvard University, undertaken as emergency measures for the duration of the war:

(1) To institute a three-term year which includes a summer term of twelve weeks, in order to shorten the time necessary to complete the requirements for the A.B., S.B., and graduate degrees.

(2) To permit students to become candidates for certain professional degrees without requiring the A.B. or S.B. degree. The basis for admission of such students is to be determined by the Graduate Schools.

(3) To admit women as candidates for degrees in the Graduate School of Design and in the Graduate School of Business Administration.

———————

In accord with these decisions, President Davis of Smith College will advise his Board of Trustees that the activities of the Cambridge Graduate School will cease in June, for the duration of the war.

Beginning June 29, all students now registered in The Cambridge School may enroll as students of the University, in many cases as candidates for the Harvard degree in Architecture and in Landscape Architecture. Students of The Cambridge School who, as college graduates, are at present candidates for the Smith College degrees in Architecture and in Landscape Architecture have the choice of completing their requirements for these degrees or of becoming candidates for Harvard degrees, subject to the requirements of the University.

———————

Students should understand that neither institution is bound to continue the policies here outlined beyond the war period. They are strictly emergency measures undertaken for two purposes: to permit students to complete their education in the shortest reasonable time, and to avoid wherever possible unnecessary duplication in educational programs.

— — — — — —

Mr. Frost will meet students in the lower drafting room on Wednesday, February 4th, at twelve o'clock, to discuss these matters further and to answer questions.[3]

On the same day, February 4, Mr. Frost sent a letter to The

Cambridge School Alumnae. He summarized the history of The Cambridge School, stressing its experimental nature and praising the people who had been a part of an interesting educational experiment. He reviewed the relationship with Smith College since 1934 and also commented on the effect of war upon all educational efforts. Not until near the end of his letter did he inform the alumnae of Harvard's decision to admit women to the Graduate School of Design and added the remark that "Smith College will collaborate in these efforts by requesting Harvard to take over these students of The Cambridge Graduate School at the end of the present academic year." His closing sentence was typically optimistic, though he may well have had some regrets and mental reservations when he wrote: "If now it seems advisable to transfer these responsibilities to Harvard, we may do so with a clear conscience and with the utmost confidence."[4]

On February 5, the Dean of Harvard University sent President Davis the exact wording of the vote that admitted women to the Graduate School of Design — for the duration of the war — and enclosed a draft of a news release for the following Monday[5]. A day or so later, President Davis formally notified all of Smith College, including the Graduate School in Cambridge, as follows:

> "On February the 3rd, Harvard University authorized its Graduate School of Design to admit women as candidates for the degrees of Architecture and Landscape Architecture for the duration of the war. In accordance with this decision Smith College announces the termination of the Cambridge School as a Graduate School of the College at the end of the academic year."

Now all the necessary announcements had been made: The three-cornered chess game was finished.

Reaction to Closing the School

Reaction to the devastating news varied. The Cambridge School faculty had known what was coming for several weeks and its members had time to adjust to the situation and to accept the inevitable. Earlier, their reaction had been one of disbelief and then generally one of disappointment, touched perhaps by resentment at the suddenness of Smith's decision. The 1941-42 official catalog had been issued almost a year before, and it included not only scheduled dates for that year but also for the 1942 Summer School and for the opening of the academic year 1942-43, September 21st. Certainly, no one had foreseen such an abrupt end to studies and jobs at The Cambridge School. Following the lead of the Director, however, the faculty tried to be objective and to dwell on the advantages of the unexpected turn of events. It must be remembered, too, that more than half its members were a part of Harvard University as well as The Cambridge School.

The students had been given very little time to absorb the full impact of decisions that, in some instances, would change the course of their lives. It is regrettable that no record was kept of the noon meeting with Mr. Frost on February 4, or at least that it is not part of the archival material on hand today. A few persons who remember the School during that period describe the students' reaction as one of bewilderment at first, then incredulity, and finally a satisfied, even jubilant, acceptance of a situation that could allow them to become a part of Harvard, such a widely known prestigious institution. In his presentation of the three-cornered arrangement that had made this possible, Mr. Frost stressed the advantage of the new plan. This must have meant some inner conflict and considerable compromise for one who, through his long teaching experience, had become convinced that women were best trained separately from men, though with equal opportunities, and whose dreams for the future of The Cambridge School had just been shattered. The wording of the February 4th notice was somewhat misleading in stating that students "may enroll" at Harvard, when it would have been more accurate to say "may apply for enrollment." Whether the notion that The Cambridge School students were officially transferred *en bloc* to the Harvard Graduate School of Design, an erroneous notion that became widespread later on, stemmed from this February 4th meeting is possible but doubtful. It is more likely to have spread from the letter Mr. Frost wrote to the alumnae the same day. (See Appendix K.)

Some of the alumnae probably had heard rumors of change, and there was little doubt that the "neighboring institution" presumably showing an interest in The Cambridge School was Harvard. That seemed no surprise or cause for alarm, as Harvard had been interested in The Cambridge School in one way or another since 1915. Less than four years before, however, the alumnae, as well as the faculty and most members of The Cambridge School Board of Trustees had opted for integration with Smith College instead of Radcliffe, partly because they feared that if Radcliffe were chosen Harvard would have too strong a voice in decisions about professional training at The Cambridge School. The alumnae were not upset at the news that Harvard was about to admit women to the Graduate School of Design. They may even have considered the decision a small victory in which they had played a part. They were disturbed, though, by its temporary nature, and they questioned the phrase "for the duration of the war." When they learned that Smith was going to close The Cambridge School and that the decision to do so had been made by postal vote after little, if any, discussion of long-range academic effects, their reaction was quite different. It can only be compared to a swarm of hornets whose nest has just been hit by a small boy. Letters and telegrams poured into President Davis's office from all over the country, and none of them were complimentary. A comparable deluge of mail arrived at Mr. Frost's office, but the pervading tone of those letters was not so much one of anger but of deeply hurt pride. The alumnae who were practicing had found their training to be reliable and a help to them in facing the realities of the professional world. They had faith in future possibilities for women who were similarly trained. Many of them, particularly those in the Boston area, had worked very hard indeed to keep the School running during some of its roughest times, and they were emotionally as well as professionally attached to it. They were satisfied with being a part of Smith College, but they were singularly apathetic toward being boosters for the Harvard Graduate School of Design. The alumnae wanted Mr. Frost to tell them whether the news was true and whether the decision was final or was, perhaps, reversible. They asked what had gone wrong with the 1938 agreement with Smith.

On February 28, Mr. Frost wrote to the alumnae again, explaining in greater detail the sequence of events that had led to his earlier letter.[6] Nothing in the second letter was new to anyone in Cambridge, but it was a good summary of events for the far-flung alumnae. He told his former students that giving them advance information would have required informing the thousands of Smith College alumnae, too. He reminded them that war affected everyone and that he had not been an entirely free agent during the past few months. He couldn't resist inserting a little sermon on responsibility, so he wrote:

> "So long as you are a student it is your privilege to be served in every way that education can serve you, and your responsibility is limited. When you have finished your education,...upon you falls a burden of responsibility... to assure your successors better privileges than you enjoyed....Past memories are as dear to teachers as to alumnae, but for teachers the school period is never over....As we mature we cling tenaciously to the status quo. Youth on the other hand is eager for new worlds to conquer.... The students must come first, and I believe our decision will prove advantageous to them."

Mr. Frost's letter of February 28 was written just after he had been notified that the Smith College Board of Trustees, at its meeting on February 20, had voted

> "to ratify the action taken by postal vote to terminate the Cambridge School of Architecture and Landscape Architecture as a graduate school of Smith College at the end of the present year, with the understanding that the vote, couched in legal phraseology, be passed again at the meeting of the Board in June." [No one had any doubts as to the outcome of the June vote.] The Board also voted that

"the administrative staff continue as long as necessary in summer but not beyond September 1st," and that the "record files be transferred to Mr. Frost's office at Harvard."[7]

Last Days of The Cambridge School

At 53 Church Street, projects and classes progressed as usual. Work on the drawings and models of The Plan for Smith College received the highest priority, as the project had to be finished by June. In April, Mr. Frost asked for and received permission to use the School station wagon to go to Detroit, where he read a paper at a meeting of the Association of Advanced Architectural Studies. Throughout the Spring, many minor requests were approved by the College. Although most of the books, photos, and prints in The Cambridge School Library went to the Art Department Library at Smith, the New York Alumnae Group bought some 200 to 300 books. Some of the Boston alumnae bought part of the furniture. All money received from these small sales was turned over to the Smith College Treasurer.

In the inexorable way of all calendars, the page marked June 1942 suddenly showed itself as the current month, and the business of operating a school became the business of closing it. On all fronts, little chores had to be faced and completed. Arrangements were made for Smith College trucks to transfer furniture, equipment, books, etc. to Northampton. Whatever the College did not want was to be given to the Red Cross, the next occupants of the building.

At the end of the month, some of The Cambridge School students became absorbed in the challenge of a summer term at Harvard, others left Cambridge altogether, planning to transfer to other institutions or to go into war work near their homes. Life for the students who went directly to Harvard changed very little. They were accustomed to the Collaborative Summer School begun in 1940. About the only physical change required by the regular attendance of women at the Graduate School of Design was the remodeling of an office in Robinson Hall to provide separate (but equal, we hope) toilets for the women. Actually, the space used for this purpose was more than adequate as wash room, cloak room, dressing room, health room, even sometimes as lunch room on rainy days. Perhaps the contractor had a surplus of black glass on hand, as he used it lavishly. The *art nouveau* decor and ample space were in sharp contrast to the simple and somewhat crowded facilities at 53 Church Street. (It must have startled staid old Robinson Hall.) Proportionately, the number of women at Harvard was not very high during World War II, nor has it been in the almost forty years since then, among either students or teachers. Elizabeth Barnes Bird was the first of The Cambridge School students to be graduated in 1943 and was also the first woman to receive a degree from the Harvard

Graduate School of Design.

Since most of the members of The Cambridge School faculty came from the Harvard Graduate School of Design, the closing of the School meant a relatively minor adjustment of teaching schedules, but the men deplored the loss of the greater flexibility they had had in teaching at The Cambridge School. Of the faculty members who did not also teach at Harvard, four persons stand out as having served the School most consistently over many years — Edith Cochran, Carol Fulkerson, Eleanor Raymond, and Albert E. Simonson. After the School was closed, Edith Cochran continued and expanded her already established private practice in Cambridge, where she lived not far from Harvard Yard. Carol Fulkerson worked at Harvard's Radar Research Laboratory, as well as maintaining his own private practice in landscape architecture, until 1945. At that time he and Si Simonson and Elizabeth Pattee (from the Lowthorpe School) went to Providence to teach in the newly established Lowthorpe Department of Landscape Architecture at the Rhode Island School of Design. When Si Simonson relinquished his first post as Head of the Lowthorpe Department to become Dean of the School in 1947, Carol Fulkerson became Head of the Department. He was succeeded by Elizabeth Pattee. Since his retirement, Carol Fulkerson has lived in nearby Barrington, Rhode Island. Eleanor Raymond continued her active and distinguished practice in the Boston area for many years. In 1977, during an outstanding exhibition of architectural design at the Massachusetts Institute of Technology, which included some of her work, she was honored at the exhibition by a special testimonial reception called an *Evening With Eleanor Raymond*. Before going to the Rhode Island School of Design, as mentioned above, Si Simonson carried on an architectural practice in Cambridge and also lectured at Lowthorpe. After his retirement, he lived in Providence until his death in 1963. In thinking of those who contributed much to the life and integrity of The Cambridge School, no one could forget three of Mr. Frost's administrative assistants: Priscilla Loud Simonson established sound procedures and kept the machinery at 53 Church Street running smoothly for many years. She died in Providence shortly before her husband's death in 1963. Louise Leland maintained an active and distinguished architectural practice in Louisville, Kentucky, until her death in 1956. Dorothea MacMillan Hanna quite literally worked beyond the call of duty and kept things remarkably steady during the rather trying last days of the School. She died in 1977.

For the Director of The Cambridge School and his overworked staff, the summer of 1942 held only the sheer drudgery of sorting, labeling, and packing, as well as writing inescapable reports. That is not to say that the School ended with a whimper rather than a bang, nor is President Davis' letter of December 14, 1942 to Mr. Frost an adequate appraisal of the situation. It is a brief letter and can be quoted in full:

"I am much obliged to you for sending in the final report of the Cambridge School for 1941-42. There are certainly no flowers and no tears but it is probably better so, and I think you have hit the note which should be equally acceptable to the alumnae of the school and to the college. With many thanks and all good wishes, Sincerely yours."

The usual signature "Herbert Davis" does not appear on the archival copy of the letter, which was probably signed by his secretary in his absence.

Actually, there may have been no flowers, but there were many unshed tears, along with acceptance of the inevitable. Though Mr. Frost probably was glad to have more time for his job at Harvard, in 1942 he worried about many of the persons who were having to adjust to new conditions. He was satisfied that his faculty members would eventually find situations to their liking. He thought that the resourceful Mr. Geary could find another job, perhaps staying on in the same building under new management. He was deeply concerned, however, about his friend Ralph Berger, whose talent for dealing with embryonic topographic models and tired books was unexcelled. Though he had been an invaluable asset to The Cambridge School, Mr. Berger had passed the age when other jobs in his field were readily available. After some months working as a cabinet maker in Cambridge, he retired to his sister's home in Pennsylvania.

The Plan for Smith College

It was Si Simonson who in the summer of 1942 took on the task of tying together various parts of The Plan for Smith College with a written summary of the joint project and recommendations for its implementation.[8] He reported briefly on the history of The Plan itself, the points of view of the designers who worked on it, and some of its disadvantages as well as its general merit. Then he discussed more fully conditions on the campus at that time and what might be anticipated in the next twenty-five years. He emphasized the importance of keeping the general character of the campus, which he thought could be accomplished by sound zoning of certain areas, and of designing new buildings "as simply and straightforwardly as possible." He concluded by saying that The Plan was intended to be flexible and was submitted "as a goal toward which future changes may be directed."

Although all records of that period indicate that the plans and models, the basic elements of the project about which President Davis had been so enthusiastic, were shipped to Smith College, probably at the same time the report was submitted, no one there now knows what became of them. Of the persons who normally would have had the responsibility of carrying out the plans — President Davis, D. M. Anderson, W. I. P. Campbell, Karl Putnam, and Kate Koch — only Miss Anderson and Mr. Campbell are still living. They have no recollection of ever having seen the final comprehensive plans and models in Northampton, nor do they recall the others having spoken of them at any time. No one who might have had a hand in the unpacking is still at Smith. The mystery of The Plan for Smith College, covering 1875, 1941, and 1966, probably never will be solved. Both President Wright and President Mendenhall, who succeeded President Davis, were builders at heart and added several new buildings to the campus. It is unfortunate that they had no comprehensive plan to follow, or at least to consider, and that many wise suggestions by W. I. P. Campbell were overruled by the architects in charge. However, thanks mostly to Mr. Campbell's innate good taste and his occasional reference to the rather scrappy old Anderson plans, the Smith campus today is a remarkably pleasant place. Under the guidance of President Jill Ker Conway it is likely to remain so.[9]

End of An Experiment

For the last issue of the *Alumnae Bulletin of The Cambridge Graduate School of Smith College,* dated July 1942, Mr. Frost wrote a masterly summary of the School's history, which he called "An End and A Beginning."[10] He closed his story by saying:

"We face the end of a period. For some of us it means possibly a farewell to the best part of our lives, to a period of fine adventure, and the loss of associations we loved with men and women we deeply admired....As we mark the End, we face a Beginning, in a world which needs courage and faith as never before. Our eyes must be set on new and better goals toward which we will arrive, and which we will never quite attain, but with the certain knowledge that youth will go forward always."

He commented on some, but by no means all, of the people who had contributed to the success of The Cambridge School. He also asked the alumnae to send him information that could be used to write a comprehensive history of the School. Although later, in 1943, he made notes on the early years of the School, they told the story only as far as World War I. One wonders whether the alumnae failed to respond to his plea, whether responsibilities at Harvard during World War II demanded too much of his time, or whether the story in which he was the central figure proved to be too difficult to tell. No one knew the subject better, and it is our loss that he did not write a complete history of that small institution known as The Cambridge School that affected the lives of so many persons. The many articles and letters he wrote while "the experiment" was underway, however, give us a remarkably clear picture of the changes in the training of women in two recognized professions during a period of profound as well as superficial changes, and they show his steadfast faith in women's ability to cope with the professional world.

It was not until November 29, 1945, at a meeting of the last Board of Trustees of The Cambridge School, that the corporation (The Cambridge School) was officially dissolved.[11] Attending that meeting were Henry A. Frost, Hope Slade Jansen, Walter H. Kilham, Eleanor Higginson Lyman, Bremer W. Pond, Isabel DeCourcy Porter, Eleanor Raymond, Romney Spring, and Fletcher Steele. Acting on behalf of the Trustees of Smith College they voted to have Romney Spring, Treasurer, take all legal steps necessary to clear the deed to the property at 53 Church Street and return the property to Faith Bemis Meem so that she might sell it to the Cambridge Community Federation.

The crystal ball may have been clouded when in the early days Mr. Frost wrote "No school dies if it is alive." In the eyes of many, The Cambridge School did not die a natural death through lack of enthusiasm and keeping up with the changing times, but rather it became the victim of circumstances beyond its, or anyone's control. It almost died in World War I, when few good teachers were available. World War II dealt the final blow, even though an abundance of good teachers and enthusiastic students were absorbed in their work. When the School most needed a friend in court, many of its staunchest supporters, including William Allan Neilson and A. Farwell Bemis, had left the scene through either retirement or death. President Davis was a new broom at Smith, as were several members of his Board of Trustees. They had not been part of the steady development of the School through the uncertain years of gaining recognition and authority to grant degrees, through the market crash and the depression, and they were called upon to make very hard decisions during precarious times.

No tangible evidence of The Cambridge School, as such, remains. The building at 53 Church Street, the old Dalby House and its large serviceable wing, is now the headquarters of the Joint Center for Urban Studies of Massachusetts Institute of Technology and Harvard University. The Cambridge School's long-time companion, the Lowthorpe School, is remembered today through the Lowthorpe Department at the Rhode Island School of Design. One finds no such reminder of The Cambridge School at Smith College or at Harvard, and most professional women today are unaware of the part it played in and around Harvard Yard before World War II. The spirit of this unique experiment in education is carried on by the work of its graduates.

[1] The school in Cambridge was sometimes referred to as the Graduate School but more often by its old name, The Cambridge School.

[2] See Appendix J.

[3] Unfortunately, no record was kept (or at least none is now available) of the noon meeting on February 4th. It must have brought forth many questions from a stunned group of students. As usual, secrets had been well kept.

[4] See Appendix K.

[5] See Appendix L.

[6] See Appendix M.

[7] The files remained in Mr. Frost's office at Harvard even after he retired in 1949. After his death in 1952, Mrs. Frost thinned out irrelevant material from these files, a thankless job, and sent all archival records to Smith College. Many changes had occurred at Smith during the war and postwar period, and by 1952 few persons there remembered anything about The Cambridge School. The files shipped from Harvard remained in the basement of College Hall for years. Only when basement space became critical for College records were most of The Cambridge School files moved to their appropriate home, the well-organized Smith College Archives.

[8] *A Report on The Plan for Smith College,* 8 June 1942, by A. E. Simonson of the Cambridge Graduate School is a very readable document now in the Smith College Archives.

[9] In May 1978, the Smith College Medal, a high honor, was awarded to W. I. P. Campbell for "his contribution to the college during 34 years of teaching eager students and enhancing the hills and valleys that form the campus."

[10] See Appendix N.

[11] See Appendix O.

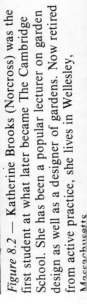

Figure 8.2 — Katherine Brooks (Norcross) was the first student at what later became The Cambridge School. She has been a popular lecturer on garden design as well as a designer of gardens. Now retired from active practice, she lives in Wellesley, Massachusetts.

Figure 8.1 — A 1978 view of the old Dalby House at 53 Church Street, the last of several homes of The Cambridge School before it was closed in 1942.

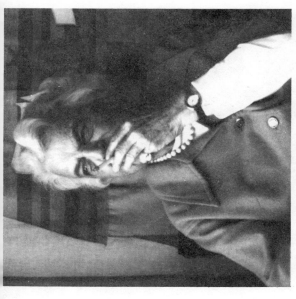

Figure 8.4 — Eleanor Raymond, architect, was an integral part of The Cambridge School throughout its entire life. She was one of the first students at the nameless school, later a professional associate in private practice with Henry A. Frost, a critic judging student solutions to design problems, an organizer and supporter of the Alumnae Association, Trustee of The Cambridge School, and in the last years of the school a Trustee of Smith College. She has retired now but still lives in Cambridge.

Figure 8.3 — A recent photo of Edith Cochran, landscape architect, an early graduate of The Cambridge School who taught landscape construction and planting design there during most of the years the school was in operation and later practiced in Cambridge under her own name.

Figure 8.6 — Cary Millholland (Parker), ASLA Fellow, worked in camouflage and map modeling units during World War II and later maintained her own office practicing landscape architecture in Washington, D.C. Here she is seen at her home on Cape Cod.

Figure 8.5 — Anne Bruce Haldeman, Cambridge School graduate whose career has been centered in Louisville, Kentucky. Her work has included designs for parks and industrial developments as well as private gardens. She also lectures on subjects related to landscape architecture.

Figure 8.7 — Clermont "Monty" Lee, one of the many Smith College students who continued her studies in landscape architecture at the graduate school in Cambridge. She has contributed greatly to the beauty of Savannah, Georgia, through her work in historic preservation and through her own designs.

Figure 8.8 — Alice Orme Smith, left, on vacation with Eleanor Jones (Poyner) not long before her death in 1980. The distinguished career of Alice Orme Smith, ASLA Fellow, included work in Beatrix Farrand's office, where with several other Cambridge School landscape architects she worked on plans for Dumbarton Oaks, in Washington, D.C. Later she practiced in New York and Connecticut. Among many honors she received were the French *Croix de Guerre* for her hospital work in France in World War I and the Smith College Medal in 1973 for "bringing men and nature into harmony in the landscape."

Figure 8.9 — Maud Sargent says she is "setting her sights on a better environment" in Connecticut, where she now practices. She was among the landscape architects who pioneered on public works projects in the Madison Square Garden Building during the 1930's. Later she spent many years working for the New York City Park Department and for city and county commissions in Pennsylvania. During World War II she was one of

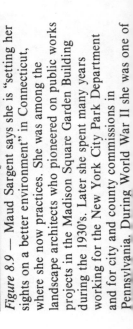

Figure 8.10 — Laura Mezitt (Russett), not only practices landscape architecture but is very active in many organizations that help to conserve and contribute to the beauty of the New England landscape. Perhaps her early feat of stitching up the fabric for a homemade airplane led to a current

Figure 8.12 — Phyllis Smith (Swayze), who as landscape architect for the National Colonial Farm in Accokeek, Maryland, has devoted most of her time in recent years to this restoration of a mid-18th century working farm. It is across the Potomac from Mount Vernon and will help preserve the threatened view from George Washington's porch and spacious lawn.

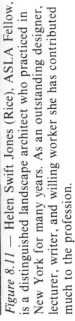

Figure 8.11 — Helen Swift Jones (Rice), ASLA Fellow, is a distinguished landscape architect who practiced in New York for many years. As an outstanding designer, lecturer, writer, and willing worker she has contributed much to the profession.

Figure 8.13 — Alice Upham (Smith), while practicing in Arkansas and elsewhere has found time to write three books on landscape architecture: *Trees in a Winter Landscape; Patios, Terraces, Decks, and Roof Gardens;* and *A Distinctive Setting for Your House.*

Figure 8.14 — Elizabeth Meade (Arthur) taught landscape and architectural design at Vassar College from 1932 to 1962, and during World War II she also taught drafting and other related courses. While teaching she carried on an active practice in New York and Connecticut. She has retired to Easton, Maryland, where she advises various organizations on local landscape projects.

Figure 8.15 — Jane Pearson (Hansen), who practices in High Falls, New York, is with Dan Smiley and onlookers examining a core from the largest sassafras tree in the state.

(Photo Courtesy of Flower and Garden Magazine)

Figure 8.16 — Peggy Pogue (Macneale) spends much of her time writing articles on landscape design and gardening for newspapers and magazines, though she has an active practice and a big family.

Figure 8.17 — Eloise Wells (Johnson) specialized in designing estates and many types of small gardens, while also spending much constructive time on her own gardens near St. Louis and in Florida.

Figure 8.18 — Ruth Smith (Bruckman) finds time for activities other than restoring old houses and gardens of the South, which she does beautifully. Some may know the Spanish garden she designed for the Condé Charlotte Museum in Mobile, Alabama, where she lives.

Figure 8.19 — Grace Hight (Kirkwood), after practicing landscape architecture in New England for some years, moved to the Middle East. Her report on her professional work in Iran, Lebanon, Kuwait, Qatar, Bahrein, Syria, and Saudi Arabia sounds like a story from the Arabian Nights. She has designed grounds and gardens for foreign embassies, government buildings, and private residences, the most recent private gardens for the King and for the Crown Prince of Saudi Arabia. Now she is practicing from her home in New Hampshire and writing a book on cultivated plants for the Middle East.

Figure 8.20 — Eunice Hull (Campbell) with her late husband, Neil, on a windy hill in New Zealand. During World War II she worked at the Boston Navy Yard and for the National Defense Council. Since then she has practiced both architecture and landscape architecture in western Canada and the Pacific Northwest. She maintains an office in Spokane, Washington, where she is the landscape architect for the Park Department and also teaches landscape Design at the Spokane Community College.

Figure 8.22 — Alice Recknagel (Ireys), ASLA Fellow, has practiced in New York for many years. She is well known as a lecturer and has taught at the Brooklyn Botanic Garden and at Connecticut College in New London. Recently she has written an outstanding book, *Small Gardens for City and Country*, which follows her earlier one, *How to Plan and Plant Your Own Property*.

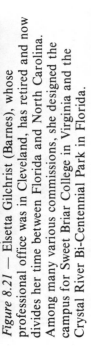

Figure 8.21 — Elsetta Gilchrist (Barnes), whose professional office was in Cleveland, has retired and now divides her time between Florida and North Carolina. Among many various commissions, she designed the campus for Sweet Briar College in Virginia and the Crystal River Bi-Centennial Park in Florida.

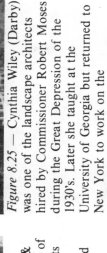

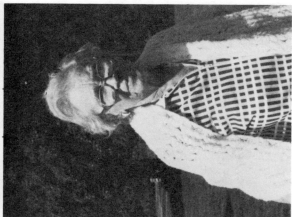

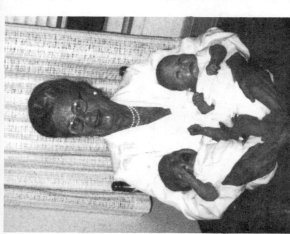

Figure 8.23 — Eleanor Jones (Poyner) with her new twin granddaughters. Eleanor Poyner is not only a landscape architect but a city planner as well, and she has the distinction of being one of the first women elected to the American Institute of Planners (AIP). Although she spent most of her professional life working for the City of New York, she now lives in Texas. From the State Legislature of Texas she recently received a citation for being "A Pioneer Among Women in the Career World."

Figure 8.24 — Helen B. Warner, ASLA Fellow, of Desmond, Eddy & Warner, Inc., was a member of one of the first firms of landscape architects to become incorporated. She has retired after a long and distinguished career in Middletown, Connecticut.

Figure 8.25 — Cynthia Wiley (Darby) was one of the landscape architects hired by Commissioner Robert Moses during the Great Depression of the 1930's. Later she taught at the University of Georgia but returned to New York to work on the redevelopment of the World's Fair Grounds. Under her own name and with colleagues Alice Ireys and Clara Coffey she practiced in New York City and upstate New York until her retirement to Bridgehampton, Long Island.

173

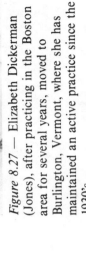

Figure 8.27 — Elizabeth Dickerman (Jones), after practicing in the Boston area for several years, moved to Burlington, Vermont, where she has maintained an active practice since the 1930's.

Figure 8.26 — Katharine Wilson (Rahn), ASLA Fellow and outstanding landscape architect. One of many Smith College students who continued graduate work at The Cambridge School, she has maintained a very active office in Buffalo, New York, for many years. She is now chairperson of the New York State Board of Landscape Architects.

(Photo Courtesy of Smith College Archives)

Figure 8.28 — William I. P. Campbell, Horticulturist Emeritus from Smith College and guardian of its campus for some forty years, was awarded the Smith College Medal in 1978, while Smith's first woman President, Jill Ker Conway (center), looked on.

Figure 8.29 — Henry Atherton Frost shortly before his death in 1952. His expression of looking into the future, perhaps contemplating the status of women in the professions of architecture and landscape architecture, is typical and was well known to many generations of former students.

Sources

The basic facts in this history came from the official records and correspondence of The Cambridge School from 1915 to 1942, now held in the Smith College Archives. The rather meager account of school activities provided by these old records is supplemented by information recently gleaned from voluminous correspondence with individuals, former students and many others, who knew the school well at some time during its existence. It is further supplemented and interpreted by my own memory of events between 1929, when I enrolled as a student of landscape architecture at The Cambridge School, and 1942, when as a member of the faculty of Smith College I was present at the closing of the school by the Board of Trustees. At that time it was The Smith College Graduate School of Architecture and Landscape Architecture in Cambridge.

Publications that I have relied on for background and a few elusive facts include: *LANDSCAPE ARCHITECTURE, A Quarterly,* American Society of Landscape Architects Publication Board, January 1925 through October 1942; *WOMEN IN ARCHITEC-TURE AND LANDSCAPE ARCHITECTURE,* Henry Atherton Frost and William R. Sears, Institute for the Coordination of Women's Interests, Smith College, 1928; *ALUMNAE BULLETIN OF THE CAMBRIDGE SCHOOL,* Cambridge School Alumnae Association, 1928 through July 1942; *THE TEACHING OF LANDSCAPE ARCHITECTURE,* Stanley White, published privately by Samuel Peaslee Snow, Auburn, Alabama, 1953; *NEILSON OF SMITH,* Margaret Farrand Thorpe, Oxford University Press, 1956; *THE GARDENS AND ARBORETUM OF SMITH COLLEGE,* Mary Mattison Van Schaik, Smith College, 1971; *FROM TIPI TO SKYSCRAPER,* Doris Cole, i press, inc., 1973; *FLO: A BIOGRAPHY OF FREDERICK LAW OLMSTED,*

Laura Wood Roper, Johns Hopkins University Press, 1973; *LANDSCAPE ARCHITECTURAL EDUCATION,* Gary O. Robinette, Kendal/Hunt Publishing Co., 1973; and *SMITH ALUMNAE QUARTERLY,* Smith College Alumnae Association, November 1938 through November 1974.

In compiling Chapters I and II, I drew heavily upon a collection of notes made in 1943 by Henry Atherton Frost. While he was jotting down a few of his memories the year after the school was closed, he must have been thinking of writing a History of The Cambridge School, but apparently he did not continue such preliminary notes after 1943. The first two chapters are a brief summary of what he remembered about the school in the early days before World War I.

APPENDIX A

Categories of Courses at The Cambridge School in 1928

1. Design

The Cambridge School considers that most problems in design require both architectural and landscape criticism, the relative importance being dependent upon the character of the problem.... Our students ...not infrequently take the same design problem and receive both architectural and landscape criticism. The point of departure...comes in the landscape program, with problems dealing strictly with the development of ground forms, which imply a greater knowledge of topography than should be included in an architectural course, and with planting design in which an architect generally receives no training and in this School only one course....

2. Construction

In landscape schools, construction begins usually with the study of elementary surveying, simple ground forms, a study of contours, cut and fill, road construction and elementary drainage. In both architectural and landscape schools it is customary to introduce a course in the construction of architectural features, including working drawings of such elements as steps, terraces, pools and walls.... The Cambridge School requires [such courses] of its students in both curricula. The point of departure here is [that] the architects continue their three-year course in [architectural] construction... while the landscape architects continue for a similar period with advanced landscape construction. By this plan, all the students... have enough understanding of the difficulties... of the profession in which they are not majoring to prevent...errors that may come through entire ignorance.

3. History

... It is no more proper nor indeed possible to divide these two subjects [architecture and landscape architecture] than it would be to consider either of them without relation to the civilization that produced the different epochs, and without relation to painting, sculpture and the minor arts. In The Cambridge School five terms...are required of all students.

4. Freehand

... The freehand courses are primarily to train the hand in the use of the pencil and brush, the eye in exact visualization of form and color.

...If the hand and eye are properly trained through life drawing, through the study of natural and architectural forms, in line, proportion and color, both architects and landscape architects should become adept in all ordinary types of freehand drawing....Any separation of the freehand courses would be considered an unwarranted expense.

5. Miscellaneous Subjects

...The miscellaneous courses include those which are...necessary as a foundation on which to build the training in design and construction, such as descriptive geometry, shades and shadows, perspective and mathematics....They include such courses as plant materials and horticulture...prerequisites of [landscape] design and planting design....[They] take only a minor position in the student's schedule, not because their importance is disregarded, but because with the short period allowed for professional training, a great deal of time has to be devoted to the courses in which continuous direction and instruction are necessary....[They also include short introductory courses in] professional practice and heating and plumbing [so that]...a student may go into an office with a certain basic knowledge in such matters.

APPENDIX B

Excerpt from The Cambridge School Bulletin 1930-1931

THE FACULTY

Design

HENRY ATHERTON FROST, A.B., M.Arch., Director of the Cambridge School.
Faculty Instructor, Graduate School of Architecture, Harvard University.

WALTER FRANCIS BOGNER, Architectural Design.
Instructor, Graduate School of Architecture, Harvard University.

KENNETH H. N. NEWTON, S.B., M.L.A., Critic in Landscape Design.

CAROL FULKERSON, S.B., M.L.A., Critic in Landscape Design.
Instructor, Graduate School of Landscape Architecture, Harvard University.

ANITA R. RATHBUN, A.B., Draughting Room Assistant.

*JEAN JACQUES HAFFNER, Architectural Design.
Architecte Diplome par le Gouvernement Francais.
Grand Prix de Rome.
Professor, School of Architecture, Harvard University.

*JOHN S. HUMPHREYS, Architectural Design.
Professor, Graduate School of Architecture, Harvard University.

*BREMER W. POND, S.B., M.L.A., Thesis Critic.
Associate Professor, Chairman of the Council of the School of Landscape Architecture, Harvard University.

*HAROLD HILL BLOSSOM, A.B., M.L.A., Landscape Design.

*WILLIAM R. SEARS, S.B., M.L.A., Landscape Design.

*ELEANOR RAYMOND, A.B., Architectural Design.

Construction

EDWARD A. VARNEY, S.B., Architectural Construction.

MORLEY J. WILLIAMS, S.B.A., M.L.A., Landscape Construction.
Instructor, Graduate School of Landscape Architecture, Harvard University.

EDITH V. COCHRAN, A.B., Landscape Construction.

BRACKETT K. THOROGOOD, Lecturer in Mathematics.
Educational Counselor, Franklin Union, Boston, Massachusetts.

History

KENNETH JOHN CONANT, M.Arch., Ph.D., Lecturer in Architectural History.
Assistant Professor, Graduate School of Architecture, Harvard University.

CAROL FULKERSON, S.B., M.L.A., Lecturer in Landscape History and Critic in Design.

Plant Design and Plant Materials

STEPHEN F. HAMBLIN, S.B., Instructor in Plant Materials.
Assistant Professor, Graduate School of Landscape Architecture, Harvard University.

MARY P. CUNNINGHAM, A.B., M.A., Instructor in Planting Design.

ROBERT S. STURTEVANT, A.B., M.L.A., Instructor in Planting Design.
Director of the Lowthorpe School.

EDITH V. COCHRAN, A.B., Instructor in Planting Design.

*GUY H. LEE, A.B., M.L.A., Critic in Planting Design.

Freehand

FRANK M. RINES, Instructor in Freehand Drawing.
Instructor, Massachusetts School of Art, Boston, Massachusetts.

ETHEL G. BARTLETT, Instructor in Freehand Drawing.
Instructor, Massachusetts School of Art, Boston, Massachusetts.

MARY GAY, Instructor in Water Color.
Instructor, Winsor School, Boston, Massachusetts.

CHARLES T. JACKSON, S.B., Lecturer in Professional Practice.

*Practitioners who give special problems and thesis criticisms.

183

APPENDIX C

Proposal for the Affiliation of The Cambridge School of Architecture and Landscape Architecture as a Graduate School of Smith College

Addressed to the President and Board of Trustees of Smith College from the President and Board of Trustees of the Cambridge School of Domestic Architecture and Landscape Architecture the proposal for affiliation reads as follows:

1. That the School be known as The Cambridge School of Architecture and Landscape Architecture, An Allied* Graduate Professional School of Smith College. That it continue in its present location which in the opinion of the Board of Trustees of the School is best fitted for the professional study of Architecture and Landscape Architecture.

2. That degrees "Master in Architecture" and "Master in Landscape Architecture" be granted by Smith College to the holders of Bachelor's degrees of recognized institutions, on recommendation of the faculty of the School upon completion of one of the two curricula offered by the School, normally requiring three and one-half years to complete.

3. That the degrees of "Master in Architecture" and "Master in Landscape Architecture" be granted by Smith College to past graduates of the School whom the faculty can recommend as having properly fulfilled the requirements outlined under No. 2, above.

4. That Certificates of accomplishment in Architecture and in Landscape Architecture be granted by The Cambridge School to students who are not holders of Bachelor's degrees upon satisfactory completion of the same curricula as those required for the Master's degrees.

5. That the administration of the School continue to be in the hands of a Council, as provided in its present By-Laws; that the Board of Trustees of the School include the President of Smith College (ex officio) and not less than one nor more than two members of the Board of Trustees of Smith College. That one member of the

Board of Trustees, representing Smith College, sit on the Council of the School, if in the opinion of the College this is desirable.

6. That Smith College assume no financial responsibility in regard to the School; that the School on its part undertake to conduct its finances and its business management in such a manner as to meet the approval of the College authorities, and always under the direction of the School Council and the Board of Trustees of the School; that the books of the School be open to the authorized auditors of the College at all times.

7. That the Council of the School, through its Ways and Means Committee and otherwise, continue to raise funds for the School's needs as heretofore; that gifts to the School for any purpose, including endowment and scholarships remain the property of the School, administered by the School Treasurer.

8. That the present By-Laws of the School be submitted to the Smith College Board for acceptance or changes before such time as the School may become an allied graduate school of the College, and that an agreement be reached as to the method to be followed in making any changes in the By-Laws thereafter.

9. That the academic direction of the School be in the hands of the School Faculty as heretofore, subject to such control from the College as the two institutions shall agree is for their mutual benefit.

---

*The word "Allied" must have been a typographical error in the Minutes, as "Affiliated" is used in all correspondence and formal documents. The School was known as an "Affiliate" until 1938, when it became an integral part of Smith College.

APPENDIX D

List of Candidates for Degrees at Smith College

June 1934

Alison, Alma	Univ. of Tenn.	M.L.A.
*Bacon, Geneva	Univ. of Mich.	M. Arch.
*Bailie, Margaret Henderson	Bryn Mawr	M.L.A.
*Bates, Dorothea Breed	Smith	M. Arch.
*Berg, Clarice Melinat	Univ. of Minn.	M. Arch.
*Blaney, Elizabeth	Vassar	M.L.A.
Bucknell, Anita Rathbun	Mills College	M. Arch.
*Burke, Ruth Bemis	Smith	M. Arch.
Childs, Muriel	Vassar	M. Arch.
*Cochran, Edith V.	Northwestern	M.L.A.
Craver, Mary	Wellesley	M. Arch.
*Dixon, Mary Newbury	Smith	M.L.A.
Fleisher, Elizabeth Hirsch	Wellesley	M. Arch.
*Garland, Eunice	Wheaton	M.L.A.
*Gilbert, Harriet H.	Vassar	M. Arch.
Gilchrist, Elsetta	Sweet Briar	M.L.A.
*Harrison, Dorothea K.	Smith	M.L.A.
*Havey, Ruth M.	Smith	M. Arch.
Hires, Linda S.	Wellesley	M. Arch.
Jackson, Frances	Smith	M. Arch.
Jones, Elizabeth Dickerman	Smith	M.L.A.
*Jones, Eleanor Robertson	Bryn Mawr	M.L.A.
*Kirkland, Grace Hight	Wellesley	M.L.A.
*Leland, Louise	Smith	M. Arch.
Lowry, Gretchen Best	Wellesley	M.L.A.
McPherson, Bertha Mather	Vassar	M. Arch.
*Meade, Elizabeth	Vassar	M.L.A.
*Millholland, Cary Blunt	Wellesley	M.L.A.

*Newton, Frances Beede	Smith	M.L.A.
Norcross, Katherine Brooks	Radcliffe	M.L.A.
*Patey, Harriette W.	Mt. Holyoke	M.L.A.
*Porter, Isabel DeCourcy	Smith	M.L.A.
*Potter, Priscilla Page	Smith	M.L.A.
Raymond, Eleanor Agnes	Wellesley	M. Arch.
*Rice, Elizabeth	Smith	M.L.A.
*Sargent, Maud	Cornell Univ.	M.L.A.
*Sawyer, Gertrude	Univ. of Ill.	M. Arch.
*Schwinck, Esther	Univ. of Mich.	M. Arch.
*Sebold, Gladys Ross	Smith	M.L.A.
*Slade, Hope	Vassar	M.L.A.
*Spring, Mary Nearing	Bryn Mawr	M.L.A.
Stearns, Anna B.	Vassar	M.L.A.
Taylor, Elizabeth	Wellesley	M. Arch.
*Watkins, M. Farnum	Radcliffe	M.L.A.
*Whitmore, Frances	Vassar	M. Arch.
*Wiley, Cynthia E.	Vassar	M.L.A.
Worthy, Eleanor White	Wellesley	M.L.A.
Wund, Sarah Owen	Vassar	M. Arch.
Wyman, Esther M.	Smith	M.L.A.

*Candidates present at Commencement.

Candidates for Degrees: 1935

Five landscape architects who had been practicing for some time and who are not included in the list above were granted degrees in 1935. They are:

Baker, Anne D.	Vassar	M.L.A.
Condict, Elizabeth Montgomery	Smith	M.L.A.
Jones, Helen Swift	Smith	M.L.A.
Lamson, Mary Deputy	Univ. of Ind.	M.L.A.
Smith, Alice Orme	Smith	M.L.A.

The other three women who received degrees in 1935 — Victorine DuPont Homsey, M.Arch., Ruth Cushman Hill, M.L.A., and Harriet

Carter, M.L.A. — had finished The Cambridge School more recently.

A comprehensive list of women who received Certificates from The Cambridge School is not available. A partial list compiled in 1932 has many familiar names, including Helen Allen, Jane L. Bailey, Eliza Birnie, Constance Emerick Bromley, Laura Cox, Mary Scott Evans, Helen Douglass French, Rose Greely, Elizabeth Clark Gunther, Elizabeth Harding, Ina C. Johnson, Esther Kilton, Felicia Doughty Kingsbury, Helen Kirby, Rosalind Spring LaFontaine, Edith Sinclair Mason, Frances Beede Newton, Esther B. Power, Eleanor Kew Pryzbylska, Mildred Rutherford, Mary Nearing Spring, Charlotte Wallum, Elizabeth Bright Weld, and Elizabeth Woolley.

APPENDIX E

Announcement to Cambridge School Alumnae about Integration with Smith College*

As of September first this year [1938] The Cambridge School ended its existence as an independent institution to become The Smith College Graduate School of Architecture and Landscape Architecture. Through the generosity of the graduate who made the Church Street property available to the School in 1928, this property has been transferred to the College. The accumulated deficit of the School is being liquidated by certain gifts, including one of $15,000 from the Albert Farwell Bemis Charity Trust. Smith College has agreed to conduct a graduate school of architecture, landscape architecture and allied subjects on the Cambridge property for a ten-year period.

It has taken twenty-three years to write the first chapter of our School history — a long period as one enters upon it, but a surprisingly short span of time as seen in retrospect. The first chapter was one of pioneering effort, and has accomplished its main objectives, including the establishment of professional curricula of high standard particularly adapted to the needs of women students, educational recognition among colleges and in the professions, and an assurance of continuity which permits the School to plan for the future with confidence.

Those of us who have worked together in the School during the past years as teachers and students shared a great advantage which will be remembered with increasing pleasure and pride as the new chapter unfolds. A school must advance with such students as ours, nor would it dare to fail utterly its loyal alumnae. It is a simple truth, sometimes not recognized, that the students make the school. To say that teachers inspire their students is but another way of saying that good teachers are made when groups of students inspire them. You who have studied at The Cambridge School will never know how much midnight oil has been burned in our efforts to quench your insatiable curiosity. As I look back over the years it seems to me that every advance has been dictated by your demand for more and better teaching. It is right that a pioneering school should face poverty during its early efforts. If it accomplishes its ends in spite of poverty there is reason to believe that the effort was justified. Had we been well endowed there must always have remained some doubt whether we succeeded because of our riches or because of our value. This is equivalent to saying that we believe the School has value.

There is always a grateful relief when a struggle is over, but success in education is never final; each step completed is but a foundation upon which to build toward the next accomplishment. Our School is still young in years, and at the very beginning of its work. The second chapter will cover naturally a ten-year period, during which we must hope so to establish its value that Smith College will look with pride upon its new graduate school as a necessary part of its educational fabric. While we shall continue to improve in every possible way our architectural and landscape curricula, and to strengthen their natural interrelation, we have another task, which is to build a curriculum in interior architecture. Here again is a pioneering effort of great interest and increasing importance. The more material side of our problem includes the necessity for adequate scholarship funds, for general endowment, for added building accommodations. The changes in teaching methods during the past ten years have resulted in need for greater draughting space per student. The changes in library requirements to include blueprints, manufacturers' samples and catalogues, demand increased space. Lecture rooms are inadequate in number and equipment. Instructors have no offices in which to work. You will see, then, that the accomplishment of the first objectives merely paves the way to the undertaking of new efforts. If with some of you there is disappointment that The Cambridge School name has given way to another, let me warn you that the spirit of the place which you knew will change only when you will it by withdrawing your interest and your loyalty. A professional school should be a part of a great institution. It is not by accident that every important graduate school in the country is in such a position. It is our good fortune that one of the greatest pioneering institutions in women's education should find us worthy. We owe much to President Neilson and to his Board of Trustees for the opportunity they have opened up for us, and we owe a debt of gratitude to our own Trustees who have guided us through so many difficulties and prepared the way for future undertakings. There are new problems to conquer and there is increased strength for the conquest.

Henry A. Frost, Director

---

*Excerpted from The Cambridge School *Alumnae Bulletin,* November, 1938

APPENDIX F

SMITH COLLEGE GRADUATE SCHOOL OF ARCHITECTURE AND LANDSCAPE ARCHITECTURE

53 CHURCH ST., CAMBRIDGE, MASS.   TRO. 3480
OFFICE OF THE DIRECTOR

September 23, 1940

President Herbert J. Davis
Smith College
Northampton, Massachusetts

My dear Mr. Davis:

I am distressed that the enclosed communication takes on such a pessimistic note. I am particularly sorry that it must go to you even before your inauguration. I have believed through a considerable portion of my life that if a man makes a better mousetrap than his neighbor the world will beat a pathway to his door, but I am becoming convinced that the neighbors are not supposed to advertise. In 1939 I talked with Mr. Neilson about the School's future. At that time he felt that he should not approve any major plan of action that would perhaps embarrass his successor, and I was in complete agreement with him. Last year my concern was such that I approached Mrs. Morrow. She felt that her mission was to keep the College functioning smoothly and to prevent a deficit, and again I appreciated her position. Thus for two years our efforts in Cambridge have had to be limited. I had hoped to spare you worry about the School during your first year in office, but I would be inexcusably remiss if I did not bring matters of such grave concern to your attention promptly, while the School is still strong and is functioning satisfactorily from an educational point of view.

I can see no other alternative than to spend a considerable sum this year on public information, or to accept during the next few years staggering deficits. I shall be glad to come to Northampton to talk with you further on these matters.

Very truly yours,

Henry A. Frost
Director

HAF:DMH
ENC

SEPTEMBER 1940 REPORT TO PRESIDENT DAVIS

General Statement

The accompanying blueprints, one headed "Attendance Table," and the other "A Graphic Chart," give the attendance record of a twenty-five year period of the School in Cambridge, and a forecast for a following three-year period, based on the present trend. Column #2, indicating the number of new students entering in a given year for professional training, and Column #4, indicating the total professional registrations for a given year, are the most important.*

The School building was planned twelve years ago for a maximum enrollment of 60 regular students. Recent changes in teaching methods, particularly the introduction of models for design problems, make 45 students a proper maximum, 50 students the limit of our accommodations, because of the greater work space required per student. The professional school loses a certain number of students yearly through graduation from its course leading to the Bachelor's degree, a few by graduation from the advanced course leading to the Master's degree, and a very small number through withdrawals for various reasons. It can enroll new students in first-year courses as candidates for the Bachelor's degree or First Certificate in architecture or in landscape architecture, and in fourth-year courses, the latter being students who have already earned their Bachelor's degree in architecture or in landscape architecture at some other institution, and who come to Cambridge for a Master's degree or a Final Certificate in architecture or in landscape architecture. The acceptance of students from other professional schools in the middle of the course — that is to undertake second- or third-year work, has not been found satisfactory, as a student is likely to lose a year by the transfer. In order, then, to keep the total professional registration at a desired level, and to assure a gradual growth, the number entering each year should be somewhat larger than the number graduating in the preceding June.

It will be noted on the Graphic Chart that for a considerable period of the School's history, the total registration included a large percentage of special students — that is, students who registered in one or two courses as auditors, but with no intention of undertaking professional study. The School is not opposed in principle to these students. On the other hand, the teaching space is limited; tuition charges for regular students are high; the faculty receives modest salaries for intensive work over long periods. It has seemed therefore only fair to concentrate all our efforts and to reserve most of our space for the regular students. The drop in special registrations during the last few years has been intentional. The time may come when it will seem desirable to offer extension courses, as is done in other schools. At present the plan does not seem feasible.

For twenty-two years the School was an independent organization, although during the last four of those years, from 1933 through 1937, it was an affiliated graduate school of Smith College, which meant simply that the College assumed no financial responsibility, but granted professional degrees to our students upon the recommendation of our faculty. During this period, with the exception of the year 1923-24, the entering classes were generally sufficient not only to balance withdrawals and graduation, but to permit some growth. From 1938 through 1940, the two years that the School has been an actual part of Smith College, registration maintained reasonable levels, although professional registration for 1939-40 was 45 as against 49 for 1938-39. On the other hand, our records for 1938-39 showed a decrease of one-third in inquiries about the School as compared with 1937-38, and the records for 1939-40 again showed a decrease of one-third from the inquiries of 1938-39.

For the academic year 1939-40, 11 students were graduated. The new enrollment for 1940-41 should be at least 16, and preferably 20. The estimated total professional enrollment for 1940-41 is 33, as against 45 for 1939-40; and the estimated enrollment of new students is 7, as against 11 for 1939-40, and 15 for 1938-39. In June 1941 we should graduate 14 students. With a possible loss of 2 from withdrawal during the year, it is reasonable to assume that 17 students will return for 1941-42. If registration next fall does not decline further, assuming perhaps 7 new students plus possibly 6 of those graduating in June 1941 returning for the Master's degree, we would have a total professional registration for 1941-42 of 30. Similarly, for 1942-43, assuming a slight upswing and 10 new students enrolling, the total professional registration may well drop to 23 if no special effort is put forth by the School. While the effect of our small entering class this year will be felt seriously next year, the full force of the deflection in registration will strike us in 1942-43. A larger entering class next year would still leave the second- and third-year classes very small in numbers, because of the small number registering this fall and the large graduating class next spring. A large entering class again in 1942-43 would leave us with a woefully weak third-year group for that year, and possibly with no students returning as candidates for the Master's degree or the Final Certificate. One small entering class hurts the School for three years; two years of small registration are dangerous. If it continues for three years it may be disastrous.

In a professional school of design there should be a certain amount of competition in design courses. Less than 6 students taking a given problem is unfortunate. 12 students in a problem make a good number, both for competition and for comparison.

The overhead for 20 students is the same as for 45. Teaching expenses may be cut somewhat for the smaller group, but it is evident that all the courses required for a proper training must be given, whether for one or for a dozen students. Teaching in the design professions is expensive, because so much of the work is tutorial in nature. If registration is allowed to fall to a small number of students, the deficit between expense and income will increase rapidly. Standards will suffer in spite of all efforts. Discouragement will result in the faculty, dissatisfaction among the students. Rumors of failure will spread among other schools, to our very great harm. Lost headway should be overcome promptly.

Possible Causes of the Present Condition

(1) The severe drop in registration has come so unexpectedly this year that it seems almost a reflection of the unsettled times. It is probably true that educational resistance is greater than usual. On the other hand, a glance at our graph shows a strong upward trend during the first World War; only a slight leveling off during the minor depression of the early '20's; a strong spurt ahead up to 1930; a slight deflection during the early part of the major depression; but a prompt recovery and upward trend. In 1935-36 we again dropped somewhat in professional registration, and apparently until this year were leveling off to the number that we feel the School can accommodate — between 45 and 50. Present world conditions may be a contributing cause; not, I believe, the main one.

(2) Educational competition has undoubtedly increased of late years. In 1915 a certain number of technical institutions were coeducational by charter. Generally they did not favor women students in their professional departments. Almost the first students in this School were a group of four who transferred from the Massachusetts Institute of Technology. Today co-education is favored in the very schools that formerly opposed it. The change is logical. The general attitude toward women and the attitude of women has changed in the past twenty-five years. They are accepted in business and in professional life, and are preparing for such activities in increasing numbers. Many of them have made excellent progress. Educational competition may be a contributing cause, and should be considered seriously.

(3) Tuition. The average tuition for professional schools is $400.00 a year or less. This School and M.I.T. are, so far as I know, the only two professional schools in architecture or in landscape architecture charging a tuition of $600.00 a year. Undoubtedly students will not pay a high tuition unless the reputation of the School warrants it. Public information about the School becomes of the greatest importance.

(4) Recognition. This School has been recognized by the American Society of Landscape Architects for years. When the Association of Professional Schools of Landscape Architecture was founded some years ago, this School was one of nine throughout the country considered worthy of being a charter member.

In architecture the School has never been recognized officially by the American Institute of Architects, because of a lack of any basis of continuity — i.e. endowment. Until the School was taken over by Smith College it was not possible to make even an attempt for recognition by the A.I.A. and the School was not greatly disturbed, because enrollment continued satisfactory and graduates practiced successfully, passing state board examinations where required. Lack of recognition by the A.I.A. undoubtedly gives an excellent opportunity for a whispering campaign.

(5) Lack of public information. For the past two years the School has not been active in this work. The loss of the School name and individuality, which had been built up assiduously for twenty years, may be more serious than was anticipated when the School became a part of Smith College. Exhibitions have not been sent out and schools have not been visited by our faculty as much as formerly. An active campaign of public information is essential.

(6) Failure in teaching. This seems hardly worth considering. The history of the School is the history of a continuous effort to improve courses and the method of presenting subject-matter. The student turnover is small, which would indicate reasonable satisfaction. Students generally complete the three-year curricula, and an encouraging proportion return for the fourth-year work. Education in the two professions is undergoing a change greater than at any time in the past twenty-five years. The schools apparently are leading rather than following the practitioners. It is an exciting time to be teaching, particularly in Cambridge, where the three schools — Harvard, Technology, Smith — may be considered very definite leaders in the more modern approach to design. It may be that we have not capitalized on this as thoroughly as we should. There has been in our minds a certain distaste for showmanship in education. That our present training is basically sound, and that the teaching is better today than at any time in the past, seems true beyond doubt.

(7) Scholarships. The School has not enough scholarship aid to offer its students, particularly in view of the high tuition.

Conclusion

I find myself unwilling to accept the defeatist attitude that present world conditions are primarily responsible for the poor enrollment this fall. When educational resistance is strong, the best schools, if they are known, should get the students. We are not well enough known. I am inclined to think it was a mistake in 1938 to give up the School name. Smith College is justly famous for its cultural training, but does not, I believe, register in people's minds for technical courses. Nor do I wish to propose a lower tuition at the present time. To do so when numbers are falling off is too obvious. If we can get to the point where all applicants cannot be accepted, and the School is nationally recognized, it might then be wise to reduce tuition to the general level in the East, which is $400.00 On the other hand it might under such conditions seem unnecessary to do so. The best way to meet educational competition, granted excellence of curricula and of staff, is to be very active in public information.

The School is unique in its program and in some of the methods by which it carries out its work. It is designed entirely for women students whose approach to professional training is naturally different from a man's approach. It meets women's needs as no coeducational school can do. Its students are extremely loyal both in the School and after they leave, the best possible proof that the School is appreciated. The School has therefore something definite and valuable to offer.

I urge the following program for the current year:

Item

1. Name: on catalogues, papers and other printed matter:

Smith College
The Cambridge School of Architecture
and Landscape Architecture
A Graduate Professional School of
Smith College

2. A carefully prepared exhibition of students' work to go to all important women's colleges, junior colleges and preparatory schools in the East, as far north as Bennington, and south to Washington, D.C., and Sweet Briar in Virginia. This exhibition would have to travel by car, because the models are all too delicate to travel by train. The exhibition would be accompanied by a member of the staff who would give talks on the work of the School.

Item	Estimated Cost

Requirements:

Car of station wagon type (if purchased)	$900.00	
Special shelving and cases for exhibition	75.00	
Garage, 12 months	120.00	
Insurance	150.00	
Mileage — expense and depreciation, 5000 miles at $.04 a mile	200.00	
Travel expense for staff	250.00	
Cost of exhibition (beyond budget expenditure)	350.00	$2045.00

3. A photographic exhibition of students' work, to be sent through the Middle West and to the West Coast, prepared for train transportation. To a large extent this exhibition would be photographs of drawings and models prepared for the exhibition under item #2. A member of the staff should visit western schools.

Requirements:

Cost of exhibition	250.00	
Transportation of exhibition	200.00	
Train and travel expense for staff	500.00	950.00

4. Illustrated catalogue. A college catalogue is generally dry reading. Some of the leading professional schools are issuing catalogues with illustrations, well-designed printing and covers. I suggest such a catalogue.

Requirements

Cost (beyond amount already budgeted)	$350.00	
Other printed matter	250.00	
Mailing, etc.	200.00	$800.00

5. Scholarships. To offer for 1941-42 a scholarship having a value of $400.00, applied to tuition, to one graduate of each of the following colleges: Bennington, Bryn Mawr, Mt. Holyoke, Radcliffe, Vassar, Wellesley. (Smith is otherwise provided for by two full scholarships and the Hurlbut Fund).   2400.00

To offer for 1941-42 a scholarship having a value of $400.00, applied to tuition, to one graduate in architecture or in landscape architecture from each of the following coeducational institutions: Universities of Oregon, California, Illinois; Iowa State College, Pennsylvania State College, Cornell University.

2400.00   4800.00

Total appropriation needed $8595.00

A School of 45 full paying students (tuition $600.00) would give us annual tuition income of $27,000. The cost of operation is estimated as $36,000, making an annual operating deficit of $9,000. A drop to 20 full paying students would give an annual tuition income of $12,000, an estimated cost of operation of $30,000, making an annual operating deficit of $18,000. Unless the School is permitted to make a vigorous campaign this year, I very much fear that by 1942-43 we may be reduced to 20 students, a lowering of standards in spite of our best efforts, and a very discouraging uphill struggle to win back the position we have held in the past.

Henry A. Frost
Director

---

*Author's Note: Reprints of the two blueprints mentioned are not attached, as they are virtually illegible. For the reader of the 1980's, the information portrayed graphically is adequately covered in the text.

APPENDIX G

SMITH COLLEGE GRADUATE SCHOOL OF
ARCHITECTURE AND LANDSCAPE ARCHITECTURE

53 CHURCH ST., CAMBRIDGE, MASS.   TRO. 3480
OFFICE OF THE DIRECTOR

October 11, 1940

President Herbert J. Davis
Smith College
Northampton, Massachusetts

My dear Mr. Davis:

At our conference last week you asked for a record of "General
Expense" of the Graduate School for the past five-year period. It
may be interesting to you to review complete figures of expense
and income over a longer period. The School was from 1915 to
1924 strictly a private school. In 1924 it was incorporated as an
educational institution under Massachusetts laws, with a Board of
Trustees. The enclosed figures are for a sixteen-year period from
the academic year 1924-25. They are taken from annual reports
and the amounts are allocated approximately as is done today by
the Treasurer's office at Smith.

In the four-year period 1924-28 the School was in rented quarters.
"Housing" was therefore largely rent, which included janitor's
service in whole or in part. During that period there was an
operating loss of some $10,000, and fairly heavy "General
Expense" in the first and fourth years of the period.

The five-year period 1928-1933 represents the first five years in our
present School, which was purchased and altered for our use by a
graduate of the School. The Trustees felt that a rental of $4,000 a
year could be paid, hence a great increase in expense under the

"Housing" column. A considerable expense for 1930-31 and 1931-32 under the "Administration" column, during which period a business manager was installed, disappears with his withdrawal. In that five-year period a considerable "gain" for 1928-29 represents a drive to pay the deficits for the previous four-year period. From 1929 through 1933, operating losses of varying amounts occur again. "General Expense" was high approximately every other year, and a glance at the "Total Income" table indicates considerable activity in raising money. A portion of the "Total Income" over "Tuition Income" was due to rebates, at first of a portion and gradually of the entire rental charge, when it was proved that the School income was not sufficient to pay these charges.

The five-year period 1933 through 1938 shows definitely lower "Administration" and "Housing" figures, and with the exception of two years of the period, low "General Expense" figures. It will be noted throughout this chart that high figures in the "General Expense" column are generally accompanied by or directly followed by increase in "Total Income". At the end of 1933 (I think) the School property was transferred to the Corporation, the owner taking back a mortgage for her protection, but without interest charges. During this period also it was possible to transfer a large part of the School's indebtedness into notes held by individuals interested in the School who had no thought of personal gain. This proved later of great advantage to the School. The final year of this period, 1937-38, should not be regarded as typical. Educationally the School was never more successful; financially, perhaps never in poorer condition. The faculty made most generous sacrifices in salary cuts, accompanied by increased efforts. The School was committed to only about $5,000 in salary payments, with the understanding that it would pay beyond that amount as conditions warranted.

During the latest period, two years, 1938-40, the School has been a part of Smith College. We have attempted to adjust expenses and income to the allocation employed by former bookkeepers.

The percentages, as you will note, have been kept in line fairly reasonably. It has been our contention throughout the School history that the "Instruction Expense" should be the largest item in relation to the total budget. The School became a part of Smith College entirely free of operating debts. The losses of 1938-39 and 1939-40 are therefore current losses. "Instruction" expense and "Tuition Income" up to the summer of 1940 include summer school expense and income. The summer school generally showed a gain of from $500 to $1,000, largely because no portion of the operating expenses were charged against it except actual salaries of teachers, and actual course expense. When we decided to collaborate with Harvard last year in the matter of the summer school, it was felt that the advantage to the School over a long period might offset the slight loss of income. The first collaborative summer school seems to bear out this belief. 1938-39, our first year as a Graduate School of Smith College, was only a ten-month year, so that 1939-40 is the first twelve-month period as a Graduate School.

Under the column "General Expense", in which you were particularly interested, you will note that in 1938-39 and 1939-40 the amount allocated to this jumps considerably. The reason is that the sum representing unsupported scholarships granted, and charged against us as an operating expense, was placed in that column, as there seemed to be no other place to put it. The figures therefore in parentheses are the actual amounts allocated to public information.

Referring again to our conference on Saturday, it was suggested that I was asking for twice as much as I expected to get for public information. May I say that I am not asking for anything. I am telling you, to the best of my ability, based on my experience, exactly where the School stands at the moment, and exactly what I think the dangers are for the future. As my report suggested, I have not yet been able to satisfy myself as to the causes. They may be much more deeply rooted than I suspect. My thought in the matter is that they are to a large degree related to the condition of the times. Almost all of the reports I hear are similar. Many schools are suffering a slump in registration. I am told at the University here that the only school which has shown any gain this year is the School of Design, and we know that registration in several of the other graduate schools has fallen off considerably. In the School of Design at Harvard we are feeling that this is a time when we should make a particular effort in public information, because we cannot foresee what the next few years will bring. We suspect that schools will face greater difficulties than they are facing this year. We feel therefore that the best-known schools will probably be the ones which will come closest to filling their quotas of students. That is my feeling also in regard to the Smith School. If the money is available for the program that I have outlined, I believe it would be an investment to use it in the way that I suggest. If on the other hand you and your Trustees feel that I am in error in the matter, I shall be very glad to follow your advice. It is my hope that the decision can be made promptly, because whatever we do should be started as soon as it is possible to do so. May I say once more that I am distressed at the necessity of causing you this extra trouble during your first year at Smith.

Sincerely yours,

Henry A. Frost
Director

HAF:DMH
ENC

Year	Administration	%	Housing	%	General Expense	%	Instruction	%	Total	Income Tuitions	Income Total	Gain or Loss
1924-25	$4072	25	$3313	22	$1699	10	$6634	43	$15718	$10768	$11309	L $4409
1925-26	4102	22	4285	23	451	3	9493	51	18361	14533	16574	L 1787
1926-27	4974	21	5075	21	454	2	12829	55	23332	18628	22261	L 1071
1927-28	5439	20	4230	16	1570	6	15733	56	26972	20872	23692	L 3280
1928-29	5954	18	9731	29	1246	4	16740	49	33671	29855	43724	G 10053
1929-30	5546	16	9737	28	1174	3	17945	52	34402	21260	33829	L 573
1930-31	8423	23	9859	26	819	2	18467	49	37568	21125	33275	L 4293
1931-32	7472	20	9409	25	1746	5	18336	49	36963	16840	27376	L 9587
1932-33	4410	17	7152	27	281	1	14468	55	26311	17180	23327	L 2984
1933-34	5429	18	4341	15	575	2	19561	65	29906	21783	25374	L 4532
1934-35	4544	18	3107	13	744	3	15963	65	24358	21105	22849	L 1509
1935-36	4793	20	3080	13	1961	8	14027	58	23861	16702	26878	G 3017
1936-37	4036	16	3018	13	339	2	16418	69	23811	20181	20424	L 3387
*1937-38	2600	14	3044	16	2090	11	11210	59	18944	21800	23470	G 4526
**1938-39	6931	19	4567	13	†3787 (675)	11	20364	57	35649	22047	22736	L 12915
1939-40	8130	21	3143	8	‡4175 (1350)	11	23082	60	38530	19293	20974	L 17556

*Not a typical year. No salary charged for Director. Instructors' salaries greatly reduced.
**First year as a School of Smith College. Because of difference in fiscal year, was a 10-month year.
†$3112 was scholarship expense — scholarships granted beyond funds available.
‡$2825 was scholarship expense — scholarships granted beyond funds available.

APPENDIX H

THE CAMBRIDGE
GRADUATE SCHOOL OF SMITH COLLEGE
ARCHITECTURE AND LANDSCAPE ARCHITECTURE

53 CHURCH ST., CAMBRIDGE, MASS.   TRO. 3480

October 9, 1941

President Herbert Davis
Smith College
Northampton, Massachusetts

Dear Mr. Davis:

Reporting for the month of September, our bookkeeper shows me
a statement of net tuitions to Smith of $9,601.00, as compared
with $7,597.00 last year for the same period; scholarships of
$2,875.00 as compared with $1,487.00; gross tuitions of $12,000.00
as compared with $8,897.00; laboratory fees of $176.00 as
compared with $128.00; registration fees of $230.00 as compared
with $60.00. The trend, as you will see, is definitely upward, and
while part of this can be attributed to present-day conditions, our
experience being that in times of upheaval the School always
increases in size, part of it can also be attributed definitely to the
publicity work. The registration fees of $230.00 would indicate
only twenty-three new students. As a matter of fact there are
twenty-eight, but three of these have at some previous time been in
the School, their absence being of sufficient duration so that it is
proper now to consider them new students again.

Believing definitely that the time to strike is when the iron is hot, I
am bending every effort to increasing the enrollment of new
students next year over this year's, and have set as my goal thirty-
five. This means intensive work during the entire year, and will
take me away from Cambridge considerably. I am looking forward

to the time after the war when there must be a slump. It seems to me therefore that the higher we can get the registration during these (for us) good years, the less we shall feel the drop when it comes later on.

September was a very busy month in publicity. I made two trips to Louisville, Kentucky — one round trip by car, some 2,300 miles, and one trip by car to Louisville from which I returned by plane in order to keep my class appointments in Cambridge. The exhibition had a very good reception in Louisville by the local chapter of the American Institute of Architects. I gave there three lectures; one to the architects, one at the University of Louisville, and one at the Louisville Collegiate School, which sends students to Smith. I then moved the exhibition to Oberlin and gave a lecture there. About the twentieth of the month I return to Oberlin to dismantle the exhibition, and had planned originally to bring it directly to Cambridge. Since then the University of Indiana has asked for it after the Oberlin showing. I am in some doubt, because of the mileage and time limitations, whether we can accept that invitation, but I plan to do it if it seems feasible. With all our activity it seems reasonably safe now to say that the deficit for this year should not be greater than it was for last, in spite of added expense which we have had to incur. My hope, of course, is that it may be less than last year. Obviously I must raise a good deal of money for scholarships.

The Smith plan is coming along in a very interesting manner. We are held up on the general planning of the campus because we have not yet received the topographical survey, which I had understood the engineers would have ready the first of October. I have written Miss Anderson, however, asking her to send it to me at the first opportunity. We are, on the other hand, planning certain buildings, among them a chapel and a possible future theatre. A little later we shall start on dormitories and the science building. I have taken the liberty of writing to Professor Wells, Jones and Slocum asking for an appointment on the 13th or 14th of this month with Miss VanMeter, representing the School, to talk over the ideal plan for a building to meet their needs. A copy of the letter I have written is enclosed for your information. When

Miss VanMeter has assembled the facts, she will bring them back to Cambridge, and then Professor Perkins, who will direct that problem, will undoubtedly go to Northampton before he gives it out for a final talk with these professors. It may be that during the problem he will want to meet with them again, and certainly if not then, he would be glad to discuss the building with them after the students have turned in their solutions. I hope this is not going to be a burden to your faculty. You will see from the enclosed letter that I have written to the effect that it is purely student work and is not to be taken too seriously.

You spoke to me on the telephone about having the exhibition at Smith. I do not know how definite you feel about this. I can say, however, that we are completely scheduled now through the middle of March. There is a possibility of routing the exhibition South in May, which means that if we do take it to Smith this year, it should be in the latter part of March or sometime in April, perhaps directly after the spring recess. If we do have the exhibition there, it will require a gallery, as so much of the work is shown on folding stands. Please do not think that I am trying to press you in regard to this.

Sincerely yours,

Henry A. Frost, Director

HAF:DMH
ENC

APPENDIX I

SMITH COLLEGE
NORTHAMPTON, MASSACHUSETTS

OFFICE OF THE PRESIDENT

November 28, 1941

Mr. Henry A. Frost
53 Church Street
Cambridge, Mass.

Dear Mr. Frost:

Many thanks for your letter of November the 25th. I have no doubt that the publicity which we have indulged in so far has brought satisfactory results in increasing the registration of the school and I understand at the moment that you are almost over-full. Nevertheless I think it would be very injudicious to do anything which will actually increase the deficit of the school at the end of the current year. You may have heard that we have lately been considering the question of the School for Social Work which has hitherto been carried on with very slight expense but which will probably run at a deficit in the future. We have decided to assume this small deficit for a few years because we feel that the school is a contribution to the present emergency. During the discussion many references were made from the outside and from the members of the Board of Trustees to the expense of the Graduate School of Architecture. I am much afraid that unless we can substantially reduce the present deficit the Trustees will decide to give up the school at the earliest possible moment and I think you ought to know of this danger and take it into account in connection with all proposals for added expense.

I am delighted to hear of the progress of the plan and I think your suggestions for a committee consisting of Miss Raymond, Mr.

213

Putnam and Miss Anderson is a very good one. Miss Anderson told me recently that she intended to bring up the question of her status here at the next meeting of the Board. You will know what that means.

We have one other important problem for you in connection with our plan. We are about to announce next month the appointment of a new Dean and as she will be bringing a family with her the present Dean's house is much too small. Here is a real problem because in the long run we perhaps should not expect often to have a Dean who would require so much accommodation and it might, therefore, seem inadvisable to enlarge that particular house on that spot.

It is, however, an attractive position and rather suitable for a Dean's residence and I should like to know whether it would seem possible to you to make some additions there on the side which faces the President's house. There is a rather nice drop in the land towards the lake which would offer some pleasing possibilities but it is a queer old place and has been much added to already. I understand that there is a plan for new dormitories to take the place of Park House. I will ask Mr. King to send these plans to you to consider. Maybe I had better come down some time and see what you are doing and have a talk about some of these problems. I shall be away next week in the other direction but could possibly work out something after that.

Yours sincerely,

Herbert J. Davis

APPENDIX J

SMITH COLLEGE
NORTHAMPTON, MASSACHUSETTS

OFFICE OF THE PRESIDENT

January 14, 1942

Dr. Kendall Emerson
136 E. 67th Street
New York City

Dear Dr. Emerson:

During a discussion recently concerning the Smith College School
for Social Work it was pointed out that the Smith College
Cambridge School of Architecture and Landscape Architecture in
Cambridge, which we finally took over in 1938, has been a very
much more expensive luxury, and under present circumstances
would almost certainly continue to operate at a deficit of anything
from $12,000 to $18,000 a year. The following are the actual
figures:

OPERATING DEFICITS

	Capital	Current
1938-39	$ 627.68	$12,913.75
1939-40	—	14,946.71
1940-41	3,229.99	19,581.60
	$16,857.67	$47,442.06
		16,857.67
Grand Total		$64,299.73

I have recently had a good deal of discussion with Mr. Frost, the
Director of the School, to try and discover ways of reducing this
very heavy financial drain, but it would be impossible to do more
than make some small economies and there is little prospect of
obtaining any endowed funds. Under the terms of the original

215

agreement it would be necessary to operate the School for another six years before the property at 53 Church Street, Cambridge, becomes the possession of Smith College. I am told that at present it has a market value of probably not more than $35,000. The actual personal property which belongs to the School was acquired by the college by bill of sale dated October 10, 1938. The Hurlbut Scholarship Fund has a value of $10,220 but the college agreed to award a full tuition scholarship of $600 annually which really adds almost $300 to our annual expenses.

There is now a strong probability that as the result of emergency measures being taken by a neighboring institution which would provide this professional training equally well (and indeed at a lower tuition fee) the Cambridge School would be no longer required. The Director informs me that under these circumstances he would advise us to close the School at the end of the present academic year. I am writing to ask whether you approve of this, although it would entail the return of the land and building at 53 Church Street to the donor, Mrs. Faith B. Meem, and the return of the scholarship fund to Mrs. Hurlbut. Would you also be willing to give me power to act and to refer the details to the Committee on Finance and Investments to be settled at their meeting in New York on January the 23rd. I had an opportunity of discussing the matter with President Neilson who entirely approves of the proposal since he feels that under these circumstances the School will have fulfilled its purpose and needs our support no longer.

Very sincerely,

Herbert J. Davis

APPENDIX K

THE CAMBRIDGE
GRADUATE SCHOOL OF SMITH COLLEGE
ARCHITECTURE AND LANDSCAPE ARCHITECTURE

53 CHURCH ST., CAMBRIDGE, MASS.   TRO. 3480

February 4, 1942

To the Alumnae:

Since 1915, over a period of twenty-seven years, it has been my privilege to report to you at intervals on the progress of the School. Some of you may remember that early in our undertaking I stated that this was an educational experiment which would require not less than twenty-five years. In the beginning the experiment was threefold — to demonstrate whether women were fitted to undertake technical training; to determine whether they could use such a training advantageously in the practice of their profession; to discover whether the effort was of sufficient importance to assure continuity of training.

Reviewing the quarter century, it is possible to say that all our objectives have been accomplished. The intangible assets so necessary in any such pioneering effort were ours in abundance — a faculty that continuously sacrificed personal advantages to the success of the common effort; excellent and enthusiastic student material; loyal graduates who proved their worth in professional practice; a far-sighted Board of Trustees, ever patient in condoning our failures, courageous in estimating the future. In 1934 when Smith College made the Cambridge group an affiliated graduate School and offered to grant professional degrees on the recommendation of our faculty, we felt that the experiment was completed except so far as continuity of training was concerned. In 1938 when the action of Smith made the Cambridge School an

217

integral part of the college, subject to its regulations, with a right to share its resources, it was reasonable to assume that we could regard the School as established, and could look forward to a period devoted to strengthening and developing our curriculum. At that time there was some regret on the part of the alumnae that we had given up our independence. Those of us intimately concerned with the School have always maintained that the unit in education is the student, that the school is the vehicle by which the student is served. In our opinion education fails completely whenever this fact is ignored. The thought behind a school will persist so long as it serves a need.

Education in the main is conservative. Such questions as the acceptance of coeducation, particularly in the graduate and professional levels, of the shortening of the span of time required between high school and the completion of graduate studies, have aroused divided opinions which in normal times warrant long debate. War on the other hand is a period of emergency during which decisions are crystallized rapidly. Some of these decisions undoubtedly are hysterical, others are the result of logical thought which a crisis intensifies. At present education is faced with many added problems. It must move with certainty at accelerated speed. It must place a limit on debate when logic demands action. Wasted effort and unnecessary duplication have no place in its program. Since December seventh, colleges and universities have acted with a speed that indicates a long preparation for such an emergency. Harvard University has authorized its graduate professional schools to admit as candidates for their degrees students who have not received an A.B. or B.S. degree. Thus the principle of a shorter period of study is accepted, with faith that the details can be worked out. To further shorten the period of study during the emergency, most departments and schools of the University have established the three-term year. The four-year college curriculum will be compressed into two academic years and three summer terms, each of twelve weeks, and professional education can be similarly compressed.

On February third the Harvard Board of Overseers voted to admit women for the duration of the war as candidates for degrees in the

Graduate School of Design and in the Graduate School of Business Administration. In principle therefore a second problem of contention is disposed of for the period of our emergency. On February twentieth President Davis will advise his Board of Trustees that Smith College will collaborate in these efforts by requesting Harvard to take over these students of the Cambridge Graduate School at the end of the present academic year.

I am making this report to you at the first moment I am permitted to do so. I submit that we in Cambridge who share your loyalty for the School have sought to serve your best interests in the past to the full extent of our abilities. If now it seems advisable to transfer these responsibilities to Harvard, we may do so with a clear conscience and with the utmost confidence.

Henry A. Frost
Director

HAF:DMH

APPENDIX L

HARVARD UNIVERSITY
CAMBRIDGE, MASSACHUSETTS

DEAN OF THE UNIVERSITY   TRO. 3480
MASSACHUSETTS HALL

February 5, 1942

President Herbert Davis
Smith College
Northampton, Massachusetts

Dear President Davis:

I write to say that the Overseers approved the plan for admitting women to the School of Design. The exact form of their vote was as follows: "Voted, upon the recommendation of the Faculty of Design that, for the duration of the war, women be admitted to the Graduate School of Design as candidates for its degrees, upon the same terms as those applied to men."

I enclose a draft for a news release which Mr. Calvert Smith and I would like to have in final form on Saturday if that is possible so that it may be given out for the papers on Monday. We are always afraid of "leaks" in news of this sort. We realize, however, that you may wish to have no publicity until after the February meeting of your Board of Trustees. If this is so, we shall do our best to hold the news until you give us the green light.

I hope we have correctly represented the connection of Smith with the Cambridge School and the motives underlying the recent action.

Cordially yours,

George H. Chase

P.S. I hope it goes without saying that we shall welcome your corrections or suggestions.
G.H.C.

ENCLOSED DRAFT FOR NEWS RELEASE

On February the 3rd, Harvard University authorized its Graduate School of Design to admit women as candidates for the degrees in Architecture and Landscape Architecture for the duration of the war. In accordance with this decision Smith College announces the termination of the Cambridge School as a Graduate School of the College at the end of this academic year.

The property on Church St., Cambridge will be then returned to the donor in accordance with the deed of gift.

APPENDIX M

THE CAMBRIDGE
GRADUATE SCHOOL OF SMITH COLLEGE
ARCHITECTURE AND LANDSCAPE ARCHITECTURE

53 CHURCH ST., CAMBRIDGE, MASS.　　　　　　　TRO. 3480

February 28, 1942

To the Alumnae of the Cambridge Graduate School of Smith College:

I have been asked to give you a résumé of events during the past two months which resulted in my letter to you on February 4th. It cannot be done in a few words, so I must ask your patience.

On November 25th I had occasion to write President Davis on various school matters. On November 28th Mr. Davis replied, and in speaking of a decision arrived at in regard to the School for Social Work, he wrote, "During the discussion many references were made from the outside and from members of the Board of Trustees to the expense of the Graduate School of Architecture. I am much afraid that unless we can substantially reduce the present deficit the Trustees will decide to give up the school at the earliest possible moment, and I think you ought to know of this and take it into account in connection with all proposals for added expense."

This was the first intimation I had that the Smith Board was contemplating such a decision. We had been impressed and grateful for the generosity and cooperation of the College in regard to our budgets and our plans for publicity. On the other hand, realizing as we all did that war was imminent, I fully expected a sharp curtailment of expense. It would be necessary and entirely proper.

On December 2nd I wrote President Davis as follows, "In regard to the other matters in your letter" (the possible closing of the school) "I am not entirely surprised, but feel that they need very careful discussion as soon as may be convenient for you." For the rest of the month, however, always a busy one in the school, I was kept so occupied that it was not until December 30th that I could go to Northampton. My conference with Mr. Davis on the 30th convinced me that Smith was considering seriously whether they could continue the school. It will be realized that between December 2nd and 30th came the attack on Pearl Harbor, our declaration of war, and a great activity not only in the Government and in business, but also in educational centers. Institutions with trained advisers are far better able to forecast events than are ordinary individuals, and that they had been preparing for some time became apparent throughout the month of December in the rapidity with which conservative educational bodies were departing from long-established traditions and making decisions which recognized the emergency. I discussed the Smith decision as I understood it with members of the Cambridge School faculty, and we agreed that we could not attempt any operation of the school on the basis that existed before we joined Smith.

It is a fact that for some years the School of Design at Harvard has discussed at intervals the admission of women. I have believed that it would come ultimately — although probably not during my teaching life — because women are proving themselves desirable students. On the graduate school level I believe that in principle universities should not discriminate between men and women, although in practice I realize that discrimination may be necessary sometimes because of inequality of preparation, and perhaps of aptitude. During December in the School of Design at Harvard, as in so many other schools, academic discussions were giving way to practical decisions. As a member of the Smith faculty, and because I was directly responsible to the President, it was proper to inform Mr. Davis of the changing attitude toward coeducation in the School of Design at Harvard. As a member of the Harvard faculty and responsible to Dean Hudnut, it was incumbent upon me to inform him of the decision which was crystallizing at Smith. It became apparent that the Smith decision would be inevitable because of the necessity of conserving resources in preparation for an emergency graver than anything our country has ever known. That this conservation, with reference to our school, might begin earlier than had been anticipated, provided Harvard decided in favor of coeducation, would be greatly to their advantage, as can be readily understood. All of you who are college graduates must believe that the institution as a whole is more important than any one department. As both decisions affected us vitally and both appeared inevitable, it was desirable that they be related.

Of the many plans and consultations that were in progress during December and January I can report only on those with which I was directly concerned. On January 11th President Davis was in Cambridge and conferred with Dean Hudnut and me. The Dean stated then that he had come to the conclusion that as a war emergency he would propose that women be admitted to the School of Design at Harvard. He was able to say that President Conant would not oppose the admission of women to the School of Design for the duration of the emergency, as candidates for the Harvard degrees in architecture, landscape architecture and regional planning. It was evident that the University could not commit itself to any statement beyond the war emergency, nor could Smith commit itself to any statement as to its course of action following the emergency. It became therefore our chief concern to assure our students uninterrupted training. The Cambridge School has grown up under the shadow of Harvard; most of us who teach, were prepared there. We have shared in building up the tradition of the Harvard School of Design. Some of the ideas we have proposed in the Cambridge School we have been happy to see assimilated into the curriculum of the Harvard School, and many things originating in the other school we have been eager to incorporate in our Cambridge School teaching. Those of us who teach in both schools believe that our experience makes us more valuable to both.

There followed some anxious weeks. President Davis was already empowered by his Board to make a final decision and following the January 11th conference, there could be no doubt that he had done so. Dean Hudnut on the other hand must await the decision of the Harvard authorities. On February 3rd the Board of Overseers of Harvard voted to admit women to the School of Design, as candidates for Harvard degrees in architecture, landscape architecture and regional planning, for the duration of the emergency.

The die was cast, and to us whose first concern must be the students now in the Cambridge School, the relief was great. My letter to you was ready, and was sent within twenty-four hours of the final decision. And then the deluge. Your letters, telegrams, petitions and conferences with me were heartening and recalled other crises in our long and not too smooth voyage of exploration and discovery. In the last analysis it is the loyalty of our Alumnae that has enabled our school to attain an enviable reputation. I can only say now what I have said in the past so many times. The school is the vehicle by which the student is served. When the interests of the school, merely as an organization, are placed above the interests of the student, then the organization fails to do its duty. Our loyalty as teachers to our students in 1915 has not abated in any succeeding year, and in 1942 that same loyalty with our added experience is more than ever necessary for today's problems. You will ask, "What of the Alumnae?" and my answer is that education is both a privilege and a responsibility. So long as you are a student it is your privilege to be served in every way that education can serve you, and your responsibility is limited. When you have finished your education, on the assumption that the experience has been invaluable, you begin to profit from that privilege as your individual talents and circumstances permit, but upon you falls a burden of responsibility which you share with the teaching staffs, to assure your successors better privileges than you enjoyed. It is not from callousness that schools seem to be concerned always with the future. Past memories are as dear to teachers as to alumnae, but for teachers the school period is never over. It must always point toward another year and another generation. The students are the novitiates. The alumnae are a part of the school organization, but they cannot always be consulted. In this instance we are a department of a larger organization, not free agents. If alumnae were to be consulted it would have meant consultation with thousands of Smith alumnae, not merely with a few hundred Cambridge School graduates. We gave up our independence in 1938 with regret certainly, but none the less gladly, because we believed future students could be better served if we did so. You maintain that the recent decision was a sudden one and I agree. It was sudden because of a grave crisis, but the idea was not new. It had been long discussed. You say it is temporary and that by it we lose all that we have gained as a school. It is temporary so far as we can tell now, but this may be so of many things that for generations we have looked upon as permanent. We may say that we have lost many material possessions, but we must remember that we gave them into the keeping of Smith College when we became a part of the college. There are many intangible things that cannot be taken from us — a sense of accomplishment in the face of difficulties, experience in teaching, loyalty to a purpose, well-trained graduates. The school has been useful. It has served a need, and the need is recognized. A new experiment is offered. Why not take it in our stride as we have so many times in the past? We have confidence in today's students, and in those of tomorrow, as we had in those of past years. Assume if you wish that this move is temporary — and I am by no means certain that you are right — if when the emergency is over, the need for a school like ours appears again, do you doubt that four walls and a roof and a group of enthusiasts will be found as they were before? And may not some of us and some of you be among those enthusiasts? What has been done once can be done better a second time. The spirit of the school did not die when we attained the apparent affluence of a home on Church Street. It did not die when we became affiliated with Smith College, nor again when our name disappeared and we became a part of Smith, as some of you feared it would. Nor do I believe it will die if this new chapter proves to be temporary. If on the other hand time proves that finally women have gained the rights of education they so richly deserve, that they are happy and successful in this latest move, you and we in Cambridge can look back at the Cambridge School in our old age, as a job well done.

Since February 4th I have interviewed all our present students individually and find them as eager to undertake this new effort as you always were in past years when new problems arose. As we mature we cling tenaciously to the status quo. Youth on the other hand is eager for new worlds to conquer. None of us have been entirely free agents during these past months. It is always so in war time. The students must come first, and I believe our decision will prove advantageous to them. Please let me explain further anything that I have not made entirely clear. A little later I would like to make some proposals looking to the future.

Henry A. Frost

HAF:DMH

APPENDIX N

Excerpt from the Alumnae Bulletin of The Cambridge Graduate School of Smith College, Volume XIV, Number 2 — July 1942

AN END AND A BEGINNING

Henry A. Frost

To a group of teachers who for many years gave their best efforts for an educational ideal, and who at intervals made considerable personal sacrifice that their common cause might approach the goal they visualized, the peremptory closing of the School in Cambridge was in the nature of a tragedy. That the feeling of tragedy extended to a large group of the Alumnae of the School was evidenced by the inundation of telephone messages, telegrams, letters and petitions that piled high on the desk of the President of Smith College on that fateful day, February 20, 1942, when the Board of Trustees was to meet and vote the end of this particular graduate school. It was perhaps impossible at that time for any of us to view the decision impersonally, as a step forward in the program of the education of women in our fields, to which Smith College had contributed generously, as the normal end of an era which had been of value in their technical training but which was no longer necessary because great institutions were finally willing to accept women on an equality with men for such training.

One of the teachers of the Cambridge School had been connected with our precarious enterprise since its beginning in January 1916. Because of this long association it seemed reasonable that he should be known as the Director, but any of you who have had teaching experience must know that such a position is but one step above that of office boy, and as we have lacked always such a useful functionary, the distinction becomes purely academic. The Secretary assumes invariably the title of "Assistant to the director," and the director then becomes automatically the rather vague and shadowy "assistant to the Assistant to the director," or, succinctly, the "yes" man. Some of you will remember Nellie J. Carpenter, others Priscilla Loud Simonson and more recently Dorothea MacMillan Hanna. At intervals such an organization as ours appoints a Publicity Director, who immediately disposes of the prerogatives of the "Assistant to the director," becoming thereby chief in command. One remembers in this truly difficult position Louise Leland and Anita Rathbun Bucknell. Such people as these and many others who have poked their fingers into our educational pie, to its lasting good, are the real dictators in our educational efforts. To them belongs much of the credit for our successes. It is hardly remarkable that the misnamed "Director" took refuge in a heavy teaching schedule.

Let me recall to you the men and women who comprised our faculty and staff during our last year, 1941-42, mentioning them in order of their length of association with the School. It is difficult to determine whether Edward Varney, Charles Killam or Edith Cochran should have the honorary title of Dean of the Faculty. Mr. Varney has served continuously from the fall of 1926, a period of sixteen years. He began with a comparatively light schedule in his first year, but his responsibilities gradually increased to the point where even we of the School, in spite of our complete lack of inhibition, hesitated to add to his load. He has a peculiar ability to give life and interest to that subject which plagues many students beyond endurance — architectural construction. He has the unique ability also to fail a student in a course and yet to leave with her the conviction that it was the only thing he could do under the circumstances, in view of her well-recognized natural intelligence. He is a teacher to whom students and faculty alike turn with confidence when building problems bother. His patience is inexhaustible. For several years Mr. Varney has carried a schedule at the School which in itself would have taxed the capacity of an ordinary man. In addition he has been very active in engineering practice with his firm, Cleverdon, Varney and Pike. He has sacrificed his personal interest for the School on many occasions.

Charles W. Killam, like the Director, began his teaching at the School in its infancy. His name appears as a lecturer in 1916-17, when he was an Associate Professor at Harvard, and for the next eight years through the year 1923-24 he continued to lecture in construction and to criticize theses. His name does not appear in our catalogue again until 1936-37, when he returned after a ten-year lapse and taught construction until the closing of the School. During the earlier period Mr. Killam became a full Professor at Harvard and for some years was Acting Dean of the School of Architecture at the University. Since he has known the Cambridge School from its very beginnings, it is a pleasure to remember that he was with us again in its later years, when the early struggles were over and the way ahead seemed clear. In spirit I have always found Mr. Killam close to the School, even when his other duties prevented his teaching there. I remember, with sympathy for him, the innumerable problems I have taken to him; his patient, careful analysis; and too, the times when I did not follow his advice and found later that he has been right.

Edith Cochran, like Mr. Varney, began teaching at the School in the fall of 1926, to help Miss Cunningham, whose schedule was becoming too heavy. She was associated in practice with Miss Cunningham until the latter's sad death in 1933, after which Miss Cochran continued her associate's practice and took over her work at the School. We have depended upon Miss Cochran for the basic courses in plant materials, planting design, horticulture and elementary landscape construction. This latter course has been required of students in both the architectural and landscape curricula. It is a "must" course for promotion to second-year work. The slogan "Pass Miss Cochran" was well known in the School. It was a rash student who tried to by-pass her. In a school where "design" had by tacit consent among the students, and some say among the design faculty as well, the right of way over all other courses, those who taught the courses which Mr. Humphreys always referred to as "baggage" had to be good. Students would gladly check their "baggage," to be left until called for.

Beginning almost as far back as Mr. Killam or myself, we have had Clement W. Geary "et al" as janitor and general advisor. He appeared in our midst when we moved from the Brattle Building to the Abbott Building in the early twenties, and trailing him always in those days was "Billy," a little dried-up old gentleman who was Mr. Geary's errand boy and who was distinguished by a black oversized derby which he always wore — even, I am sure, to bed. It rested on his ears, causing them to ride comfortably at right angles to any direction in which he happened to face. Mr. Geary is English and has all the splendid, and many of the insular, qualities of our cousins. His loyalty is without limit. His attitude toward us all, whether student or faculty, is fatherly. When he cannot see eye to eye with us, he argues quietly, peacefully, kindly. When the decision goes against him it is surprising how many times the thing gets done his way, and generally we are none the wiser. He is a man of many gifts and of great confidence. His strength and endurance seem to be endless. When we moved to Church Street, he naturally went with us. I cannot recall any consideration of the matter. He was simply a part of our organization and it would occur to no one that we could do without him. At Church Street "et al" meant Mrs. Geary and Albert Siedler. They arranged the work and then told me of the arrangement as already a fact accomplished. Between them they have kept the house and the schoolrooms swept and dusted, the paint scrubbed, and on more than one occasion have painted rooms and corridors when they felt the need was great. While we of the faculty were struggling with academic problems, I fear we too often failed to realize what Mr. and Mrs. Geary and Albert were contributing to our physical welfare.

Carol Fulkerson, then one of the younger instructors in the School of Landscape Architecture at Harvard, came to us first in 1929, to give a course in landscape history. He was so successful with the students and so obviously had an unusual ability as a design critic that when our landscape critic, Richard Sears, died in 1932, it was logical that we should turn to Mr. Fulkerson to take charge of landscape design. He took over in a transitional period. Architectural schools were drawing away from the classic tradition, were beginning to approach design from a new point of view, to which for want of a better designation the term "modern" was applied — a term which the public translated into "modernistic," much to our distress. Those of you who remember "Middlesex Village," our ambitious project of 1933-34, and two years later "Glaston," on both of which Mr. Fulkerson was the landscape critic, can appreciate how readily he grasped the new concepts and became a leader among us in the present movement. Those of you who knew also his design for "Gardens on Parade" at the New York World's Fair, and still later his design and execution of the house for Dr. and Mrs. Kirkwood, need no further evidence that in him the School has had an understanding and facile designer.

Holmes Perkins was teaching at the University of Michigan in 1929-30. It would add to our prestige to be able to say that he returned East in order to teach in our school at the beginning of the academic year 1930-31. The most we can claim is that he did return East, and did begin to teach with us at that time. It is interesting to note how many of the teachers started at our school first of all as lecturers in history and remained to teach design. Of late years, Mr. Perkins' course on the history of modern architecture has been a greatly appreciated contribution to the curriculum. His "Comparative Outline of Architectural History," first issued in 1935, and twice revised, has had a wide sale. It did not take our school long to realize that in Mr. Perkins we had a design critic of unusual ability, and as always when such a discovery was made, we began loading design problems upon him. Unfortunately for us, the Harvard School of Design made a similar discovery at about the same time, and so two institutions began a tug-of-war with Mr. Perkins the prize. He is now an Associate Professor at Harvard and has been on leave of absence in Washington since March. During the past few years, in spite of all the demands upon his time from Harvard and from his successful practice, he has given for us at least two design problems yearly, to which we have looked forward eagerly.

Our Librarian, Ralph Berger, joined us in September, 1931, when our library was growing rapidly, largely through the gifts of a graduate, who at that time added sufficiently to those gifts to pay a librarian's salary. In Mr. Berger we found not the young librarian of purely academic training who sits primly at a desk all day "shushing" conversation in the reading room, but a man of mature experience with books because of his love for them. His own library is extensive and touches on many fields. He appreciates books completely, not only for their content, but also for their design, their print and their construction. He is an expert binder and has kept the greater part of our collection in repair. He is an accomplished photographer, understanding not merely the vagaries of the lens, but the secrets of developers. His slides are of the highest quality and he has made thousands for the School. He has a thorough mastery of tools and was happiest during the years when the School maintained a shop, with power plane, circular saw, jigsaw and many hand tools, a great number of which he contributed. His work on the intricate "Middlesex Village" model was a marvel of accuracy; the many buildings at small scale turned out from wood blocks were perfect in workmanship. That the School was awarded the Gold Medal by the Massachusetts Horticultural Society in 1935 for "Middlesex Village" was due in no small part to his untiring and highly successful efforts. If after his appointment the library still seemed to run itself for a considerable part of the time, because of his many duties, the fact remains that he knew with unerring instinct where to find the material required by fifty impatient students and by a hardly more patient faculty. His knowledge of his library was photographic. He could tell at a glance if a book had been removed during his absence, and woe to the individual, whether student or teacher, who withdrew a book without signing the proper card. Truly he is a man of many parts.

Albert Simonson was abroad in 1930-31, having married Priscilla Loud, to whom reference has been made already. By this act he did not ingratiate himself with the School, and I am still amazed that he was sufficiently forgiven by September 1931 to permit him to start a course in history at the School. To this day I am not certain whether history is his first love which design serves, or whether design is his great passion and history is its handmaiden. Whatever the truth may be, he has attained marked success in both fields, and of late years has been in charge of architectural design in the School. It is interesting to note that the three designers who have been with the School during its most important period, the past ten years — Messrs. Simonson, Perkins and Fulkerson — were all trained in the classic tradition and all started their teaching careers during that transitional period of unrest when our schools were questioning the long-established methods of teaching. It is natural, therefore, that these men should find themselves in immediate sympathy with the new ideas that were emerging, and which had already made marked progress in Europe. With such teachers our school has spanned the two periods in a manner that is most gratifying. To them belongs the credit that the transition in the School was so easily made, and that the design work has been so highly successful. For the year 1942-43, Mr. Simonson is holder of the Wheelwright Fellowship at Harvard.

Samuel Hershey began his teaching with us in 1935 in freehand drawing. I remember his telling me that he did not particularly like teaching; that he was first of all a painter and that he could not let the academic interfere with creative work. By 1937 he was teaching three courses in freehand at the Cambridge School. In 1938 there was an opening in the School of Design at Harvard, to teach freehand and a course in the principles of design. In 1940 he was teaching four freehand courses at the Cambridge School, two courses in design principles and one in freehand at Harvard. This was rather a record for one who was not sure he would like teaching. It was perhaps ironical to tell him that he still had the summers free for painting. As a matter of fact, he accomplished a surprising amount of painting, his most important work during the past two years being a mural for a post office at Cambridge City, Indiana. Mr. Hershey is one of those fortunate of men, a born teacher. He loves people, particularly young people, and they on their side admire him and have a deep affection for him. I can remember that in my own school days students never said, "I am taking geology," but, "I am taking Shaler," and so today they take Hershey. His influence in our school has been great. What he teaches is not so important as the fact that he is teaching, stimulating imagination, inquiry, argument. When he left this spring, late in May, to enter the Army as a Captain in the Air Forces, in camouflage, it was a sad day for many students and for his colleagues.

Dorothea MacMillan Hanna I have referred to earlier in this report as the wielder of the big stick. On her shoulders since 1936 has fallen the detail work which, when properly done, keeps a school running smoothly. She has been a worthy successor to Priscilla Loud Simonson. My colleagues will agree that she can melt one with her smile or freeze one with her frown. To see her typewriter at rapid pace while people ask her questions, demand telephone numbers, argue with her or tell her jokes; to hear her answer correctly, laugh at the right moment and never miss a key, is something to be remembered. That she cannot type with both hands while she answers the telephone has always been a great trial to me. She does everything with such ease, this failure makes it too evident that she falls short of perfection.

One other member of our staff, Katherine Shafer Kileski, is down on our records as "accounts," and has been since 1938, when the Treasurer of Smith insisted that we have our own bookkeeper. Her duty is not merely to tell us what we have spent, but to tell us in no uncertain terms what we can spend, and to do this requires a more intimate knowledge of the entire operation of the School than any one other person in it possesses. When the monthly statements come out, whether our love is tinged by hate or our hatred by love it would be hard to say. My remembrance is that when Mrs. Kileski first came to the office, she struck us all as a most attractive, human young person whom we were going to like. But the Treasurer of the College very nearly destroyed our first impressions by giving her a motor-driven adding machine, one of those contraptions where you press a bunch of buttons and the most amazing figures pop out, unbelievable figures, which are always correct. It dominates her every waking hour. I have often felt that if I could catch that machine in an error I would die happy. Apparently I am destined to live forever. As I write this, I suddenly realize that Mrs. Kileski is responsible only to the Treasurer, not to me, nor to the faculty.

Early in 1941-42, not dreaming that the year marked our end, we planned certain changes and additions to our faculty, to lessen the burden on some members and to round out our curriculum — Charles E. Greene, on the mechanics of buildings, a course which he will give at Harvard next year; Walter Chambers, Associate Professor at Harvard, to relieve Mr. Fulkerson in landscape construction; Robert Coolidge, recent graduate of the Harvard School of Design, to assist in interior design to replace Marc Peter, Jr., who became involved in Civilian Defense and is at present in England. Those men, who taught only during the past year, would, I hope, have continued with us had the School remained in operation, adding greatly to our teaching prestige.

If on these pages I mention only the members of our organization who served the School in 1941-42, it is because I have wanted to give you the picture as it was at the end. With the exception of the men mentioned in the preceding paragraph, the individuals I have enumerated have been with the School long enough to be regarded as its permanent staff. They are the ones responsible for its day-to-day work and for its larger plans. They are the ones upon whom the School depended to assure a proper continuity in the teaching. They bore the burden. On our records are the names of some fifty other men and women who have taught at different times, many of whom, had the School continued, would have taught again. It just happens that they did not teach the last year and I hesitate to mention any of them, much as I would like to do so, until such time as we may have an opportunity to include them all in a more complete report of this educational experiment. They all played truly important parts in the evolving of our program, and to them all we owe much.

Ours has been a remarkable school. It has bowed to no professors, no deans, and certainly not to any Director. I have never seen a group of men and women work together in such complete harmony and equality, with such common purpose, with more cheerful self-sacrifice. I have been conscious of no regimentation, of little organization, and yet lectures, conferences, criticisms, examinations have moved in their orbits without excitement or friction. It has been usually a peaceful place in which to work and still the center always of intense activity, so that it has never been humdrum. I remember once, before we became a part of Smith College, our Treasurer at the time, Romney Spring, threw up his hands in horror and said, "Man, you're bankrupt and you don't know it." The answer was obvious. We were bankrupt of course, and did know it, but we had things to do, so we must find a way around bankruptcy. We may have been at times only one step ahead of the sheriff, and so we made more plans and kept one step ahead. There was a goal to be attained and students and faculty were united in their determination to attain it. As in any worth-while activity, that goal had a way of withdrawing and expanding as we approached it. In 1924, when we were incorporated and became legally an educational institution, we reached a goal, only to arrive at another in 1928 when we were given a building which surpassed our expectations. In 1934, when we became an affiliated graduate school of Smith College, through the generous interest of President Neilson, we were tempted to feel that *the* goal had been accomplished because our students could receive degrees, but in 1938 when the President again came to our rescue and we were made an actual part of that college, still another goal had been attained, bringing with it greater economic freedom. And now in 1942 when our students are admitted to Harvard University, they become candidates for greatly-prized technical degrees. None of these goals is final. Each one is merely a little higher peak from which we set forth for other goals.

As I have said to you so many times, the student must be the unit in education, the school the vehicle that serves the student. Whether we segregate boys and girls in their preliminary education does not interest me much. I can see both sides of the argument and am content to leave the decision to those better fitted to judge. On the other hand, while we have reason to be proud of what our school has accomplished, were we at the present time endowed with millions I doubt that we could carry this phase of our work much further than we have done. The time has come in our civilization when universities must be coeducational at the graduate school level. Women must have the same rights as men in professional and research studies, and in academic recognition for those studies. It is archaic to ask whether it is a man or a woman who seeks admission to such training or to candidacy for those degrees. The proper question is whether the student, regardless of sex, is properly prepared to undertake the work.

Our school would never have started in 1916 had Harvard University and other great institutions been ready to recognize women as proper candidates for their degrees in architecture and in landscape architecture. At that time, I very much doubt that women were ready for such consideration. Since then much has happened. The whole world has changed rapidly. Young people are better trained in their earlier years. They are in my opinion more capable, better balanced, of higher intelligence, than they were in my youth. And so, in 1942, when Harvard opens its doors to women on an equality with men in our two fields, and when other universities hasten to follow suit, it seems to me that women have won their point, because they have by their accomplishment impressed the authorities that they are ready for this new consideration. We can be proud that the Cambridge School has had a hand in the matter.

It will interest you to know that thirty-six students are studying design in the summer term of the Harvard School, above the elementary class. In the first problem the result was three designs commended, twenty-four, passed, nine, failed. Of the thirty-six students, fourteen had transferred from the Cambridge School, and to this group went two of the three "commends" and only one of the nine failures.

We face the end of a period. For some of us it means possibly a farewell to the best part of our lives, to a period of fine adventure, and the loss of associations we loved with men and women we deeply admired. We all watch it go reluctantly but with gratitude that we were permitted to share in the work. And as we mark the End, we face a Beginning, in a world which needs courage and faith as never before. Our eyes must be set on new and better goals toward which we will arrive, and which we will never quite attain, but with the certain knowledge that youth will go forward always.

IMPORTANT NOTICE

This is the final Bulletin of the Cambridge Graduate School. For the future my mail address will be Hunt Hall, Harvard University, Cambridge, Mass. I hope the Alumnae will feel free to write me or drop in to see me whenever the spirit moves or whenever I can be of service.

An addressed post-card is enclosed. If you wish to be kept in touch with the progress of women's training in the Graduate School of Design at Harvard, please sign and return the card to me, because in the future, *information will be sent only to those who have indicated their interest by returning the card.*

It is necessary to compile a record of the life of the School from 1916 to 1942. This is being done with great care, and when completed could be published in book or pamphlet form. You will find a question on the card asking whether you would care to subscribe to such a record, if, as and when it is published, provided the cost were as much as $3.00-$5.00 a copy. Please indicate on the card your interest in the matter.

Henry A. Frost

APPENDIX O

The Cambridge School of Architecture and Landscape Architecture, Inc.

MEETING OF THE BOARD OF TRUSTEES

A meeting of the Board of Trustees of The Cambridge School of Architecture and Landscape Architecture, Inc., duly called by the Secretary at the direction of the President, was held at Room 1134, 73 Tremont Street, Boston, Massachusetts, on November 29, 1945, at 4:30 P.M., due notice of the meeting having been given to all of the Trustees in accordance with the By-laws.

The following Trustees were present, being a majority of the Board of Trustees:

Henry A. Frost
Romney Spring
Walter H. Kilham
Hope Slade Jansen
Eleanor Higginson Lyman
Bremer W. Pond
Isabel DeC. Porter
Eleanor Raymond
Fletcher Steele

Henry A. Frost, the President of the corporation, presided.

On motion duly seconded, it was,

VOTED: To proceed to the election of a Secretary of the corporation by ballot.

Dorothea M. Hanna was duly elected Secretary of the corporation by ballot and was sworn to the faithful performance of her duties as Secretary by Romney Spring, Notary Public.

The records of the meeting of the Board of Trustees held on June 10, 1938, were approved.

The President reported that the proposal by which The Trustees of the Smith College should take over the school of The Cambridge School of Architecture and Landscape Architecture, Inc. which was authorized by the vote passed at the meeting of the Board of Trustees held on June 10, 1938, was accepted by The Trustees of the Smith College shortly after the date of that meeting, and that under date of October 10, 1938, the President of this corporation, Henry A. Frost, and its Treasurer, Romney Spring, executed and delivered a deed of the real estate situated on Church Street, Cambridge, owned by this corporation and at the time used by it for its school, to The Trustees of the Smith College, which deed is dated October 10, 1938, and is recorded in the Middlesex South District Registry of Deeds, in Book 6245, Page 252.

The President reported that one of the terms of the proposal made to Smith College which was authorized by the vote of this Board on June 10, 1938 was that this corporation should be clear of debt at the time of the conveyance of its property to Smith College; and that in order to comply with the terms of the proposal, the President and the Treasurer made an agreement with Mrs. Faith B. Meem, who held a mortgage for $98,000 on the property of this corporation, by which Mrs. Meem discharged the mortgage, and in consideration for such discharge, a provision was inserted in the deed from this corporation to The Trustees of the Smith College that in the event that Smith College failed to use the land conveyed and any buildings upon it as a school for the education of women in architecture, landscape architecture, and related subjects, for ten years from the date of the deed, title to the premises should vest in Faith B. Meem, or her heirs if she should not be living at the time.

The President also reported that Smith College had conducted a school of architecture on the premises conveyed by this deed for several years, but had ceased to conduct the school in the year 1942 and had conveyed the property on Church Street, Cambridge, to Faith B. Meem, without covenants as to title, by a deed dated June 30, 1942. He also reported that Mrs. Meem has now agreed to sell the property to the Cambridge Community Federation, a Massachusetts charitable corporation organized for the purpose of supporting charitable social agencies in Cambridge, which is planning to use it in its work, and that in connection with the examination of the title to the property, the purchaser has requested that the conveyance of the property 53 Church Street, Cambridge, which was made by the officers of this corporation in its behalf to The Trustees of the Smith College be ratified and confirmed by a vote of this Board.

On motion duly seconded, it was unanimously,

VOTED: That The Cambridge School of Architecture and Landscape Architecture, Inc. hereby ratifies, approves and confirms the execution and delivery of the deed given in the name and behalf of this corporation by Henry A. Frost, its President, and Romney Spring, its Treasurer, to The Trustees of the Smith College dated the tenth day of October, 1938, and recorded with Middlesex South District Deeds, Book 6245, Page 252.

On motion duly seconded, it was unanimously,

VOTED: That Henry A. Frost, the President of this corporation, and Romney Spring, its Treasurer, and either of them, be and they hereby are severally authorized in their discretion to execute, acknowledge and deliver to Faith B. Meem a deed in such form as the

240

officer executing such deed may determine, conveying or releasing to Faith B. Meem any interest of The Cambridge School of Architecture and Landscape Architecture, Inc. in the land which was described in the deed from this corporation to The Trustees of the Smith College dated October 10, 1938, and recorded with Middlesex South District Deeds, Book 6245, Page 252.

On motion duly made and seconded, it was

VOTED: That the corporation should be dissolved, and that the Treasurer be authorized to take all necessary steps to render such dissolution effectual.

On motion duly seconded, it was,

VOTED: To adjourn.

Dorothea L Hanna
(formerly Dorothea L. Macmillan)
Secretary

INDEX

Names of institutions and persons not specifically mentioned in the text or acknowledgments and not included in the index may be found in the appendixes. Some records of The Cambridge School were lost; no complete list of women who studied there is available.